Methodologies in Systematic Theology

Methodologies in Systematic Theology

A Few Contributions

LOUIS ROY

WIPF & STOCK · Eugene, Oregon

METHODOLOGIES IN SYSTEMATIC THEOLOGY
A Few Contributions

Copyright © 2024 Louis Roy. All rights reserved. Except for brief quotations in critical publications or reviews, no part of this book may be reproduced in any manner without prior written permission from the publisher. Write: Permissions, Wipf and Stock Publishers, 199 W. 8th Ave., Suite 3, Eugene, OR 97401.

Wipf & Stock
An Imprint of Wipf and Stock Publishers
199 W. 8th Ave., Suite 3
Eugene, OR 97401

www.wipfandstock.com

PAPERBACK ISBN: 979-8-3852-2298-8
HARDCOVER ISBN: 979-8-3852-2299-5
EBOOK ISBN: 979-8-3852-2300-8

VERSION NUMBER 06/03/24

Contents

Acknowledgments | vii
Introduction | ix

1 A Chronological Overview of Christian Thinking | 1
  The Bible and its Variegated Reception | 1
  Patristic and Monastic Theology | 5
  The Scholastic Mind | 7
  Theology and Modernity | 10
  Varieties of Twentieth-Century Theology | 13
  Concluding Remarks | 16

2 Principles of Catholic Theology | 17
  A Plurality of Theologies | 17
  Traditions and Tradition | 21
  Sources and the Hierarchy of Truth | 22
  Systematic Theology and Biblical Texts | 24
  Philosophy's Role within Theology | 25
  Concluding Remarks | 27

3 Augustine of Hippo | 28
  The Objective Aspect of his Methodology | 28
  Subjective Aspects of His Methodology | 33
  Concluding Remarks | 38

4 Albert the Great and Thomas Aquinas | 39
  Albert the Great, the First Medieval Aristotelian | 39
  Thomas Aquinas, the Great Synthesizer | 42
  An Instance of Medieval Scholasticism | 49
  Concluding Remarks | 53

v

5 Friedrich Schleiermacher | 54
Questions and Method | 55
Interpretation: Grammatical and Technical | 57
The Issue of Psychologizing | 58
Coda: Phenomenology and Hermeneutics | 59
Concluding Remarks | 62

6 Bernard Lonergan | 63
Human Intentionality | 63
Functional Specialties | 67
A First Exposé on Interpretation | 67
A Second Exposé on Interpretation | 69
Historicity versus Extrinsicism | 73
Interpersonal Dialogue | 74
Comparing Lonergan with Schleiermacher | 79
Concluding Remarks | 81

6 Paul Ricœur | 83
The Phenomenological Method | 83
The Expansion from Experience to Text | 87
The Expansion from Text to Action | 89
Concluding Remarks | 94

8 Yves Congar and Claude Geffré | 95
Yves Congar, Historian and Thinker | 95
Claude Geffré, Expert in Theological Hermeneutics | 101
Concluding Remarks | 106

Conclusion | 109
Bibliography | 113

Acknowledgments

Over the last twenty years I taught graduate courses on theological methods and on introduction to theology at the Dominican University College in Ottawa and at Providence College in Providence, Rhode Island. I am thankful to my students for their active response, including their questions and contributions to the understanding of texts that were no easy reading.

I am also indebted to Rev. Harvey Egan, SJ, my friend and ex-colleague at Boston College, and to my friend James Pambrun, at Saint Paul University in Ottawa, for having perused, each of them, half of this manuscript and given me, so generously, helpful remarks on it. I am also grateful my Dominican brother Benjamin Ngororabanga for the many books that he was instrumental in checking out for me.

This book can be used as a guidebook for teachers in theology and/or in religious studies, and also for advanced students or educated readers. Since systematic theology is my principal area of competence, except occasionally I won't venture here into other theological fields, such as ethics, spirituality, or modern psychology, although elsewhere I wrote about topics belonging to those other fields.

I follow the usual guidelines of inclusive language about persons, either by employing the plural or by alternating "he" and "she." However, in accord with biblical language, God is referred to as "he." Biblical quotations are from the New Revised Standard Version, in *The New Oxford Annotated Bible* (Oxford University

Acknowledgments

Press), at times with slight modifications. Please note that throughout this volume, unless otherwise indicated, italicization is by the authors themselves.

Introduction

In a book titled *Christian Identity and Theological Education*, Joseph Hough and John Cobb argue that theological education is "teleological," in the sense that it aims at educating students who will be ministers or teachers in church and society. In the light of this principle, Hough and Cobb move a step further, as they write, "There can be no clear unity to theological education until there is recovery of clarity about the nature of professional leadership within the church."[1] Therefore, with the help of Alasdair MacIntyre's notion of "social characters" they proceed to describe several ministerial models which have been influential in church life.[2]

Their typology about secular characters (the Manager, the Therapist and others) is informative.[3] Moreover I share their doubts about whether the several kinds of church leadership that have been inspired by those *secular* characters are the best way to shed light on the nature of *theological* education; Hough and Cobb are right in assuming that we rather need an "understanding of what it is to be a Christian community in the world."[4] And I would suggest that what should be clarified is the intellectual side of lived faith.

If we begin with the old-fashioned *fides quaerens intellectum* ("faith seeking understanding") and if we have in mind the

1. Hough and Cobb, *Christian Identity and Theological Education*, 5.

2. See Hough and Cobb, *Christian Identity and Theological Education*, 5, footnote 12.

3. See Hough and Cobb, *Christian Identity and Theological Education*, 16 and 19.

4. Hough and Cobb, *Christian Identity and Theological Education*, 19.

Introduction

contemporary connotations of the word "meaning," we can state that the human person is a symbolic animal, who spontaneously looks for meaning.[5] One desires understanding, asks about the truthvalue of what one has grasped, and deliberates regarding one's commitments. Theology is nothing else than a systematic exploration and enlargement of this quest for meaning, with sustained attention to text-interpretation, to historical oppositions and developments, as well as to the affective and normative aspects of belief. Consequently this book on theological methodologies will have much to say about the process—personal and collective—of interpretation, namely about hermeneutics.

This view of faith and theology invites us to focus, not on the *objects* which are studied, but on the inquiring *subject* that each of us is.[6] Hough and Cobb note that "disputes about method are as divisive as those about doctrine."[7] Such disputes are indeed inextricable so long as we deal only with objects.

I contend that the dialogue between historical scholarship (essential to theology) and pastoral theology (also an indispensable part of theology) would be more fruitful if a wrong conception of theory was exposed and abandoned. This inadequate conception asserts that scholarship should be principally concerned with *external* data, namely texts, artifacts, events, rituals, social structures, etc. What is then neglected is a handling of religious meanings that would be objective and universal enough to be transposable from one historical context to another. When historical and systematic theologians do not believe that historical transpositions are feasible, they mediate to their students a mass of useful information, but not an intelligible set of truths. In so doing, historical and systematic theology create an insurmountable problem for pastoral theology.

How is it that so many students have the impression that theological scholarship is "purely theoretical" and unconnected with "faith seeking understanding?" Maybe some of them are

---

5. See Roy, *Meaning in People's Lives and in Human History*, forthcoming.

6. I include the inquiring subject as religious; see the Preface to my book *Mystical Consciousness*, ix–xi.

7. Hough and Cobb, *Christian Identity and Theological Education*, 3.

Introduction

ignorant and prejudiced. But in fact many are correctly reacting against the long-lived Western illusion that real, serious scholarship must be academic in a conceptualist sense—concepts being more important than questions and insights.[8] They vaguely feel that conceptualism cannot express the religious meanings that constitute the core of human life. Moreover if so many pastoral theologians take an existentialist, emotivist, or therapeutic view of their profession, are they not backlashing against the seemingly-normative positivistic conception of scholarship?[9] And what happens when students and teachers reject the pragmatic, managerial view, which stands further away from "faith seeking understanding"? This book will therefore eschew erroneous conceptualist-line abstractions and will do much better, by building on the readers' search for meaning as they discuss theological texts.[10]

It is most important to realize that students' *knowledge* is grounded and unified in the *knowing* that they find in themselves as they have access to God in faith, as they respond to God in love, and as they pray, particularly in meditation. This unification is often called "integration" and it is much more than the acquisition of a body of knowledge. The specialist in religious education Edward Farley wrote:

> The aim of education is sometimes thought to be the transmission of knowledge concerning a content or subject matter. But when we ask about the purpose of the transmitted knowledge, we are referred to another order of aims, an order having to do with the use, function, and relevance of knowledge. Knowledge, in other words, lends itself to various agendas that attend human life, and it can improve the ways human beings

---

8. On Lonergan contrast between the conceptualist and the intellectualist, see *Insight: A Study of Human Understanding*, 717–18, and Roy, "Bernard Lonergan's Construal of Aquinas's Epistemology," 17–31.

9. On emotivism, see MacIntyre, *After Virtue*; see also Roy, *Engaging the Thought of Bernard Lonergan*, 172–81.

10. Nonetheless there are sound abstractions, which, according to Lonergan, go beyond sensible data and are "enriching" because they at the service of intelligibility, which consists of a succession of insights; see *Insight*, 111–12.

Introduction

exist in the situations of life. Human life is constituted by a succession of *situations* that call for understanding and interpretation.... Here there are not just bodies of knowledge but also basic types of understanding and interpretation.[11]

Some readers may ask, where does the author of this book stand? My answer is that I see myself, not as a traditional dogmatic theologian, although I believe in the indispensability of dogmas, which I would rather call "doctrines," after Bernard Lonergan, but as a systematic theologian in constant dialogue with pastoral theologians and with scholars who practise a hermeneutical, hence historical, approach to religious texts, as will be shown throughout my enterprise.

A caveat is nevertheless in order: In the bulk of this book (chapters 3 through 8), the treatment of each author's thought will not be exhaustive, but only bear on his methodology, as indicated by the title of the book, *Methodologies in Systematic Theology*.

My book has seven chapters.

Chapter 1 presents a chronological overview of Christian thinking: in the Bible, in patristic and monastic theology, in medieval scholasticism, in modernity, and in twentieth-century theology.

Chapter 2 spells out the principles of Catholic theology, the plurality in theology, the Tradition and the traditions, the sources and the hierarchy of truth.

Chapter 3 focuses on Augustine of Hippo, his construal of Christian existence, his view of biblical interpretation, and love as the fundamental principle of hermeneutics.

Chapter 4 introduces Albert the Great, the first Medieval Aristotelian, and Thomas Aquinas, the outstanding synthesizer of a systematic theology conceived as theory.

Chapter 5 bears on Friedrich Schleiermacher, the revolutionary innovator in Protestant theology, his questions and method,

---

11. Farley, *The Fragility of Knowledge*, 135. For an historical approach to Christian education by the same author, see his *Theologia*. I thank Hosffman Ospino, a professor at Boston College, for having drawn my attention to these two books.

Introduction

the issue of psychologizing, his principles of text interpretation. That chapter will end with a sketch of twentieth-century phenomenology and hermeneutics.

Chapter 6 deals with the eminent Protestant philosopher of the second half of the twentieth century, Paul Ricœur. We shall examine his phenomenological method, his shift from human experience to written texts, and his shift from texts to human action.

Chapter 7 expounds Bernard Lonergan's thought on human intentionality, on the historical method, and his two basic exposés on interpretation.

Chapter 8 is a study of Yves Congar's and Claude Geffré's hermeneutical contributions.

To conclude this Introduction on a practical note, I would submit the following three steps in the itinerary of theology students:

- Christian students usually begin with the *knowing* that is there in their faith, love, and prayer; this knowing, to a certain extent unarticulated, remains influential during the rest of a person's life, for good insofar as it is sound, or for ill insofar as it is unbalanced.
- This initial knowing becomes a *knowledge* developed in informal conversations or in catechesis. It is enlarged and corrected thanks to history (of the Bible and of church councils).
- The knowledge thus acquired is deepened in theology (church fathers, medieval writers and contemporary thinkers).

Such an integrative process, based on human situations and not only on historical knowledge, is far from being easy, given the numerous sources of theology, which will be identified in chapter 2. If students consent to pay the price, however, they will go beyond the hodgepodge offered by most current programs of spirituality or of religious studies. By scrutinizing great Christian texts, they will then be able to make sense of their life and of the life of others.[12]

---

12. For a bird's eye view of Christianity's interpretative traditions, see Geffré, "L'herméneutique chrétienne," 449–56.

1

A Chronological Overview of Christian Thinking

This chapter presents a tour of the numerous biblical-theological travels undertaken by Christian thinkers over two millennia. So I will briefly introduce various ways of reading the Bible and I will characterize patristic theology, monastic theology, Latin scholasticism, as well as several modern and contemporary Christian forms of thought.

The Bible and its Variegated Reception

Towards the end of the second century BCE, the translation of the Hebrew Bible into Greek was made in the Hellenistic megalopolis of Alexandria. This version is called the Septuagint (commonly abbreviated as LXX). At the same time, the writers of Wisdom literature began to use a few Greek ideas to convey their Jewish beliefs. This is a case of inculturation.

Both Philo of Alexandria and Jesus of Nazareth lived in the first century CE. The writing of the NT probably commenced with Paul's First Letter to the Thessalonians, written between years 49 and 51, and it ended with the Book of Revelation a few years before year 100.

Insofar as the identity of Jesus according to the four Gospels is concerned, there has been a huge amount of debates since the eighteenth century. Thus, along with most exegetes John Meier distinguished between:

1. "the real Jesus," namely the one that actually existed in ancient Israel;
2. "the historical Jesus" (or "the Jesus of history"), namely the representation of Jesus that is the construct of historical research; and
3. "the risen Lord," who is "the direct object of Christian faith."[1]

Meier correctly stated that the Jesus known by believers is the Christ of faith. He is also right when he claims that such faith-knowledge cannot be based solely on historical scholarship about Jesus but that faith-knowledge needs to be guided and sometimes rectified by historical scholarship. Even though historical scholarship remains incomplete and hypothetical, it offers a number of facts that are highly probable and therefore reliable. By comparison, the church councils pronounced truths that Catholic believers hold as certain.

However, it seems to me that Meier unwittingly succumbed to Locke's empiricist (or positivistic) view of epistemology and metaphysics when he asserts that the real Jesus is "unknown and unknowable."[2] Without telling so and probably without knowing so, Meier espoused a naïve realism, that is, the suggestion that we can directly perceive the real. He held a *quantitative* view of historiography, which seems to be first and foremost a matter of amassing data. Of course data are indispensable, and yet, if we want to understand individuals, do we need *all* the data about them? Is not

---

1. Meier, *A Marginal Jew*, 1–3, 21–26, and 196–200.
2. Meier, *A Marginal Jew*, 22. The same Lockean leaning is also detectable in James Dunn's contention that the figure of Jesus is irretrievable, so that an objectively authenticated Jesus is a chimera. See Dunn, *A New Perspective on Jesus*; this little book sums up the thesis of his masterpiece *Jesus Remembered*.

A Chronological Overview of Christian Thinking

a limited number of *significant* data sufficient for both historians and believers to arrive at "the real Jesus," albeit in a limited and progressing manner?

According to the critical realism espoused by Thomas Aquinas, Bernard Lonergan, and Ben Meyer, reality is reached, not by taking a good look (in this case, by visualizing Jesus), but by judging the validity of one's understanding (in this case, by finding an overall meaning in the Jesus-event—a meaning that has been corroborated by biblical scholarship and Christian faith-traditions). Scholarship and church traditions must not be set against one another; both distinct contributions must be appreciated.

John Meier (not to be confused with Ben Meyer) accurately asserted that the quest for the historical Jesus serves the interests of faith. What he should add is that faith-knowledge also helps this quest. Philosophically and theologically, his hermeneutic is inadequate inasmuch as it keeps out what it considers to be interferences from dogma—a stance that Christian theology cannot accept.

Moreover, the opposite stance must also be avoided: interferences from dogma that introduce anachronistic views into earlier epochs (for instance, into the New Testament period) and that, as a consequence, are inimical to historical mindedness. This a-historical practice is called *eis-egesis* (reading "into" the text), in contrast to *ex-egesis* (reading "out of" the text).

Meier's idea about the "unpapal conclave" in which a Catholic, a Protestant, a Jew, and an agnostic could reach an "unreligious formula of concord" is a secularist proposal that flies in the face of serious hermeneutics.[3] The pursuit of a purely secular treatment of the biblical data reduces exegesis to trivial results, that is, *merely* to facts and dates that have little to do with faith.[4]

Both believing and unbelieving exegetes know that all scholarship is theory-laden, that is, deeply influenced by various

---

3. I therefore entirely agree with Giambrone's rejection of the idea of the "unpapal conclave"; see his book *A Quest for the Historical Christ*, 3–4, 33–34, and 67, note 78.

4. See *The Interpretation of the Bible in the Church* (1994), by the Pontifical Biblical Commission, on the several methods in exegesis.

Methodologies in Systematic Theology

presuppositions about possibilities (about what they think *can* and what *cannot* happen), so that actualities are acknowledged or rejected according to what historians admit as possibilities. For better or for worse, personal and communal preferences among scholars play a major role in their methodological options and choices. As Lonergan explained, in the human sciences (in contradistinction to the natural sciences) there is no purely neutral way of handling a material that is already molded by meanings and values.[5]

Insofar as Jesus is concerned, one may want to distinguish three steps. First, all began with Jesus' own construal of what he was about—a construal he attained in interaction with Mary, Joseph, his biblical heritage, and his disciples. To understand Jesus is to understand his own interpretation of himself, which is expressed in his discourses, parables, and symbolic actions.[6]

Second, Jesus' self-understanding was communicated to his disciples. After the resurrection and the Pentecost event, their understanding of Jesus became faith-laden, that is, colored by their faith. Was their understanding merely subjectivist? I would suggest that thanks to their master's Easter appearances and the Pentecost event, his disciples got him right.

Third, in turn, our faith comes from an acceptance of their testimony. The first disciples provide us with facts and understandings about Jesus, some of which can be corroborated by historians. However we have no direct access to the historical Jesus, since our belief must be based on what his disciples preached, as recorded in the New Testament. Consequently nobody can *prove* the truth of those facts and understandings. It is up to each of us to decide whether we accept that teaching. Even though, for bright people, the act of faith requires serious thinking, including historical information, it is not the direct result of a purely rational approach.

All Christian theology must begin with the Bible. The Bible gave rise to two principal ways of interpreting: the patristic-medieval and the modern. The patristic-medieval emphasizes the

---

5. See Lonergan, *Method in Theology*, 145–47, 169, and 233–34.

6. See Meyer, *The Aims of Jesus*, 16–17 and 7–94. See also his *Critical Realism and the New Testament*, 1–16, 129–56, and 195–211.

A Chronological Overview of Christian Thinking

symbolic sense, with metaphors and allegories that are sometimes relevant and sometimes farfetched; the modern emphasizes the literal sense, with judgments of fact that are sometimes grounded and sometimes fanciful. The former is usually more profound and more helpful for the spiritual life, whereas the latter usually understands the numerous mentalities of the sacred writers much better and consequently displays a historical-mindedness. Professional theologians, catechists, and students of theology need these two approaches, which are complementary.

The Bible contains a good number of writing styles, often termed "literary genres." In his encyclical *Divino afflante Spiritu* (1943) Pope Pius XII recognized this biblical characterization. Such approaches constitute ways of receiving, understanding and presenting the word of God: narrative, legislation, prophecy, wisdom, hymnology, proclamation (*kērygma*), teaching (*catēchēsis*), exhortation (*paraínesis*), apocalypse, etc.

Patristic and Monastic Theology

Let us proceed with writings made immediately after the New Testament. We then have second-century authors, dubbed by historians "the apostolic Fathers" or "the sub-apostolic Fathers": Justin Martyr (around 100–around 165), who was a convert from Platonism; Clement of Rome (around 35–around 100) who, as pope, wrote a Letter to the Corinthians; Ignatius, bishop of Antioch (35–108), who wrote letters to the faithful of his diocese before being martyred; the *Epistle of Barnabas* (between 70–132); the anonymous author of the *Didachē* (around 100); the anonymous author of *The Shepherd of Hermas*; (around 150); the anonymous author of the *Letter to Diognetus* (late second century). The canon of Scriptures was determined around 200. Virtually all these thinkers had recourse to reason in their defence of Christian beliefs.

The patristic period, which includes the works of the Greek and Latin Church Fathers, lasted from the third to the eighth century. Almost all of the participants were bishops. Hence the enormous influence of the Bible as read in liturgical settings, with their symbolic expressions and ritualism.

The Church Fathers remained close to the biblical wordings and contents, quoting it constantly while reformulating the contents in mostly Greek and Roman non-biblical words and categories. Irenaeus of Lyon (ca. 130–ca. 200), Clement of Alexandria (ca. 150–ca. 215) and Origen of Alexandria (185–254) offer what are more overall visions of the Christian life than systematic presentations.

Systematic thinking about Christ and the Trinity began with the Cappadocian Fathers (Basil of Caesarea, 330–379), Gregory of Nazianzen (329–90) and Gregory of Nyssa, 335–95). A similar systematic thinking was moving forward in the West with Augustine of Hippo (354–430). That systematic thinking prepared the position adopted by Pope Leo the Great (around 400–461) and the Council of Chalcedon (451). Later, Maximus Confessor (around 580–662) was the only major Greek Father who knew the thought of Augustine. Most historians consider John of Damascus (676–749; also called Damascene) to be the last Church Father. He summed up the Greek Orthodox tradition.

The seven Greek ecumenical councils were held from 325 until 787) and, among the subsequent general councils in the Roman Catholic Church, the most important are the Council of Trent (sixteenth century), the First Vatican Council (nineteenth century, and the Second Vatican Council (twentieth century).

The monastic theology of the twelfth century continued to use the same Neoplatonic philosophy as Augustine, and they did theology as Augustine taught it. The Western medievals often read Augustine as interpreted by Gregory the Great, who was a Benedictine monk before becoming a pope (from 590 until 605). Most of the Western monks were Benedictines or Cistercians. Among the latter, Bernard of Clairvaux and William of St. Thierry are still widely read. In the twelve and early-thirteenth centuries the abbey of St. Victor in Paris, a monastery of canons regular, also produced remarkable theologians: Hugh, Richard, and Thomas Gallus.

A Chronological Overview of Christian Thinking

The monks and canons of the twelfth century interpreted the Bible with the same three principles as the Fathers of the Church:

- Christ as the key of the Scriptures
- The rule of faith, that is, faith as received from the apostles and their disciples
- The unity of the Old and New Testaments.

Early in the Middle Ages, that is, in the Carolingian period—named after Charlemagne, who was crowned emperor in year 800 –, the monks added another principle: the *auctoritates*, the "authorities," which consisted of numerous quotations from the Fathers of the Church.[7]

The Scholastic Mind

In contrast to monastic theology, scholasticism was an enterprise that aimed at producing a theological body of knowledge consonant with human reason. The predecessor was Boethius (480–524/525), who lived in Italy and wrote in Latin. He translated works on logic written by Aristotle and he composed original logical treatises. He thus exercised a great influence on medieval thought, especially by coining a definition of eternity and a definition of person—both definitions approvingly quoted by Thomas Aquinas.

Anselm (around 1033–1109) was a Benedictine monk who became archbishop of Canterbury His scholastic mind was keen on ordered arguments, for instance in his famous proof for the existence of God.

Peter Abelard (1079–1142) is renowned for his writings on the logic of Aristotle and of Boethius, for a book titled *Dialectica*, and for another book titled *Sic et Non*, citing texts both for (*sic*) and against (*non*) various theological opinions. Bernard of Clairvaux was adamantly against the Aristotelian and logician Abelard. The novel by Umberto Eco titled *The Name of the Rose* is indicative of

---

7. On monastic theology, see Leclercq, *The Love of Learning and the Desire for God*.

the basic motive behind the strong resistance of the monks and the Franciscans to scholasticism, which, in their eyes, represented an enormous threat to the maintenance of their Augustinian culture.

The three giants of the thirteenth century were Albert the Great (around 1200–1280), Bonaventure (1221–1274) and Thomas Aquinas (1224 or 1225–1274). Bonaventure, a Franciscan friar, remained close to monastic theology, despite occasionally borrowing concepts from Aristotle when he was teaching in Paris. After giving up his university career and becoming Minister General of the Order of Friars Minor, he joined the then current reaction against Aristotle's influence and deprecated what he thought was the Aristotelian naturalism of Albert and Thomas. However, even though he wanted to be Augustinian, he contrasted faith and reason more than Augustine by emphasizing an affective, moral, experiential and scriptural approach to the revealed realities.

Albert and Thomas built up a synthesis that undertook to integrate monastic theology and scholastic thinking.[8] They were examples of what I would call "moderate scholasticism." More will be said on them in a subsequent chapter.

By contrast, Siger of Brabant (around 1240–around 1284) represented a kind of radical scholasticism, namely what was later dubbed "Latin Averroism," because he was deeply influenced by the rationalism of Averroes, the Muslim who commented on Aristotle's works. Siger was fairly or unfairly accused of teaching a "double truth": one thing could be true through reason, while the opposite could be true through faith. He and some of his colleagues in Paris, at the Faculty of Arts, were much more interested in Greek philosophy than in Christian theology.

Here are the main characteristics of scholastic thinking:

- The world functions according to its own laws; hence a certain autonomy of science with respect to Revelation is one of scholasticism's main characteristics. The translation into Latin of Plato's *Timaeus*, a dialogue that describes the emergence

---

8. See Roy, "Medieval Latin Scholasticism," 19–34.

A Chronological Overview of Christian Thinking

of the world and analyses its features, led medievals to that discovery.

- The scholastic ideal is a collaboration between reason and faith. It was initiated by Peter Lombard (around 1095–1169), who collected "sentences" from several sources: the Bible, early Christian writers, Greek, Roman, Arabic and Jewish thinkers. That body of diverse assertions exposed inevitable inconsistencies in the Christian tradition, which medieval teachers feel compelled to try and reconcile discordant opinions by crafting logical solutions. Hence the scholastic problem-solving mentality.

- Because of the influence of Aristotle's logic, the following emphases gain momentum: the usefulness of definitions, distinctions, and divisions of any subject matter; the raising of questions and objections; argumentation enacted in disputed questions (*quaestiones disputatae*), wrestling with the dialectics of contrary opinions.

- Noteworthy also is the Christian philosophers' openness to Jewish thinkers (for example, Maimonides, at the beginning of the thirteenth century) and to Islamic thinkers (for example, Avicenna, at the beginning of the eleventh century, and Averroes, at the very end of the twelfth century), with their use of *secular* philosophy (taken from Aristotle).[9]

Regrettably the prizing of symbolic discourse, as prior to systematization, hence respected by the scholastics, diminished at the end of the thirteenth century. With Henry of Ghent (around 1217–1293) and Duns Scotus (around 1266–1308), philosophical and theological thought became conceptualistic, that is, a method that emphasized concepts, which obscures the role of questions and insights.[10] It also excessively used logic, done in a virtuoso manner, with subtlety rather than profundity. Consequently in the

---

9. See Roy, "Scholasticism," 1085–88.

10. See Roy, "Bernard Lonergan's Construal of Aquinas's Epistemology," 17–31.

fourteenth century a split developed between academic teaching and spirituality.

We observe also a neglect of the Bible; for instance, we don't have any biblical commentary by Scotus—which means that either he never lectured on biblical texts or, if he did, these lectures on biblical texts were not considered significant in the fourteenth century. The last important medieval philosophers were the empiricist William of Ockham (1285–1347) and the nominalists, in particular Gabriel Biel (around 1420–495), who influenced Martin Luther.[11]

Unfortunately John Capreolus (about 1380–444) and other late-medieval Thomists stopped commenting directly on Holy Scripture and on Lombard's *Sentences*. The attention shifted to commenting on Aquinas's *Summa Theologiae*, in which the Angelic Doctor had purported to sum up biblical and sentential assertions.[12] Thus Catholic theology continued to move away from the Bible.

Theology and Modernity

The three principal Reformers of the sixteenth century were Martin Luther, Ulrich Zwingli and John Calvin. Along with Desiderius Erasmus, they were influenced by humanism, repudiated scholasticism, and held the Bible as the only normative source of Christian thinking.

At that time, beginning with Melchior Cano, Catholic theologians no longer started with questions, as was done in the Middle Ages, but with theses that were presumably "proved" by quoting biblical, patristic and conciliar sentences taken out of context. Dogmatic theology—a new designation—"replaced the inquiry of the *quaestio* by the pedagogy of the thesis. It demoted the quest of faith for understanding to a desirable, but secondary, and indeed,

---

11. On nominalism's influence upon Luther, see Roy, *God: Polarities in Language*, forthcoming, chap. 8, section titled "The Influence of Nominalism."

12. Capreolus's principal work, *Four Books of Defenses of the Theology of St. Thomas Aquinas*, is generally known as the *Defensiones*.

A Chronological Overview of Christian Thinking

optional goal. It gave basic and central significance to the certitudes of faith, their presuppositions, and their consequences."[13]

Dogmatic theologians remained content with repeating Aquinas's doctrines with a conceptualist mind that centered on concepts rather than on acts of understanding. By so doing, they remained confined within Duns Scotus's conceptualism. They engaged in otiose disputations, whose approach consisted in multiplying distinctions that threw little light on their topics. They were not interested in the valid insights of the Protestants or in the new questions posed by modernity. Their refutations of their adversaries were most of the time simplistic.

Since the eighteenth century there has been an uneasy relationship, and often an antagonism, between an historical approach and a faith approach to Jesus. This has frequently been called the opposition between the Jesus of history and the Christ of faith. Many Enlightenment thinkers—for instance Gotthold Ephraim Lessing—pointed out that the church doctrines were different from what Jesus had actually said and done. In this they were right, but they drew a wrong conclusion as they pitted the results of their historical research against the Christian views that developed after the resurrection of Jesus. Because they assumed that any addition to the original Jesus was a distortion of his thought, they rejected conciliar dogma.

Traditional scholastic Lutheranism yielded to Liberal Protestantism, illustrated by Friedrich Schleiermacher and his successors, which was influential mostly in Germany from 1800 until about 1920.[14] This trend was dubbed "liberal" because it accentuated theologians' free thinking according to a rationalist bend that had accepted Spinoza's elimination of the supernatural. They saw religious consciousness as more important than the Scriptures and

---

13. Lonergan, "Theology in its New Context," 50.

14. For a contrast between the seventeenth- and eighteenth-century Protestant orthodoxy and Schleiermacher, and between the latter and the post-World War I theologians of the dialectical theology (or the theology of crisis), see Braaten, "The Heritage of Dogmatics," in volume 1 of *Christian Dogmatics*, 36–43.

the great general councils. More will be said about Schleiermacher later in this book.

Insofar the first half of the nineteenth century is concerned, the Catholic Romantic theology of Tübingen endeavored to reconcile Thomism with aspects of liberal Protestantism. Towards the middle of that century, Josef Kleutgen rejected the Kantianism of that liberal Protestantism; it was the birth of neo-scholasticism, which played a key role at the First Vatican Council.

At the same time, Louis Veuillot and others in France forcefully defended the authority and infallibility of the pope. Because it extolled faith at the expense of human reason, their position was called "fideism." In Protestant countries, there arose, against the view of European Enlightenment, a return to Holy Scripture, namely a "fundamentalism" that purported to hold the Bible as the fundament of faith. Unfortunately it consisted and still consists in a literalist reading of the Bible, that is, in biblical segments wrongly construed, without taking their contexts into account.

In the nineteenth century, John Henry Newman successfully addressed the problem of the development of dogma.[15] In *An Essay on the Development of Christian Doctrine*, he insisted that the distinct contributions of scholarship and church traditions must be appreciated and not set in opposition to each other. He demonstrated that the normative developments of doctrine in the Catholic Church—which began with St. Paul—are a legitimate case of "faith seeking understanding" (*fides quaerens intellectum*, as St. Anselm put it). Consonant with this stance, one could say that the desire to understand better what one believes leads to inculturation, namely to expressing the Good News in the categories found in particular cultures.

Furthermore Newman sowed the seeds of a novel approach in fundamental theology, which spread little by little in France after 1900. His *The Grammar of Assent* masterpiece employed philosophy to justify the complementarity of real and notional apprehensions, that is, of living faith and theology.[16]

---

15. See Newman, *An Essay on the Development of Christian Doctrine*.
16. See Newman, *An Essay in Aid of a Grammar of Assent*.

A Chronological Overview of Christian Thinking

In 1893 Maurice Blondel defended his innovative thesis titled *L'Action*, which delineated a phenomenology of human life as logically necessitating an openness to Christian revelation.[17]

Varieties of Twentieth-Century Theology

At the outset of the twentieth century, modernism in France and in England clashed with Roman anti-modernism. The exegete Alfred Firmin Loisy, followed by a few theologians, stressed individualistic experience, which became a radical relativizing of the Church's fixed dogmas.[18] In 1890, another exegete, Marie-Joseph Lagrange founded the École biblique in Jerusalem; much later, several components of his modern biblical scholarship were accepted by pope Pius XII in his encyclical *Divino afflante Spiritu*, which I mentioned above.

Both Newman and Blondel considerably influenced twentieth-century Catholic theology, especially the Jesuit School of Lyon-Fourvière and the Dominican School of Le Saulchoir. A few years before the Second World War, a Western Patristic *ressourcement* took place at Lyon-Fourvière (Henri de Lubac, Jean Daniélou and Hans Urs von Balthasar). In 1943, members of that Jesuit School launched the first volume of the collection « Sources Chrétiennes » at the Dominican Éditions du Cerf in Paris. In the two decades before the Second Vatican Council, Marie-Dominique Chenu, Yves Congar and others published studies in the history of theology.

The other important Catholic movement in twentieth-century theology was the transcendental approach of Joseph Maréchal, Karl Rahner, and Bernard Lonergan, all of whom sought to reconcile Thomism with some aspects of modern thinking.[19]

From the 1920s to the 1960s in the Protestant churches, Karl Barth and Emil Brunner vigorously repudiated Liberal

---

17. See Blondel, *Action (1893)*.

18. See Roy, *Revelation in a Pluralistic World*, 77–78.

19. By Maréchal, see *Le point de départ de la métaphysique*. Excerpts translated into English are offered in *A Maréchal Reader*. By Rahner, see *Foundations of Christian Faith*.

Protestantism; this repudiation has been called "Protestant neo-orthodoxy" and is now called "post-liberal theology" at Yale University. For Barth, Liberal Protestantism amounted to a mere philosophy of religion unfaithful to divine revelation. By contrast, his method consisted in obeying the word of God, which he conceived as received and proclaimed in church every Sunday. The style of Protestant services is oratory, rhetorical, and consisting principally in sermons and hymns. Assuredly Barth's writings shed much light upon the contents of Christian beliefs. Von Balthasar's treatment of dogma resembles Barth's, except that he was neo-patristic.[20] In this context, I must also mention the remarkable Slav neo-patristic Orthodox thinkers (around 1850–around 1950): Bukharev, Bulgakov, Chestov, Soloviev, Stăniloae.

In Latin America, Gustavo Gutiérrez inaugurated liberation theology in his *Teología de la liberación* (1971)[21] and Clodovis Boff proposed an impressive methodology of praxis.[22]

More recently contextual theology has become fashionable; it has adopted the hermeneutical accent on human historicity, namely the "internal factors" that are required for any adequate theology. According to Stephen Bevans, five *factors* must play a role; they are:

- The incarnational nature of Christianity: given that the Son of God became flesh, the Christians must continue the incarnation process by taking into consideration specific cultures.

- The sacramental nature of reality: given that the sacramental amounts to concrete realities (Jesus himself, religious symbols events in history), Christians naturally adopt such symbols.

---

20. On von Balthasar and Barth, see Roy, *Revelation in a Pluralistic World*, 94–101 and 121–29.

21. See Gutiérrez, *A Theology of Liberation*. See also Roy, *Meaning in People's Lives and in Human History*, forthcoming, chap. 4, section titled "Gustavo Gutiérrez's Contribution."

22. See Boff, *Theology and Praxis*.

A Chronological Overview of Christian Thinking

- The nature of divine revelation: given that it consists in interpersonal relationships between God and human beings, faith is construed as a succession of divine self-communications.

- The catholicity of the Church: given that catholicity tends towards universality, it preserves the particular and the local while being potentially inclusive of the whole human race.

- Placing the Trinity as the center and source of theologizing: given the fact that the Trinity contains inner relationships between the divine persons, theology has the duty to embrace all human cultures with their relationships, events, sufferings and joys.[23]

Bevans' *models* are equally five, yet without corresponding to his internal factors. His models are: (1) Anthropological; (2) Praxis; (3) Synthetic; (4) Translation; and (5) Countercultural.[24] They resemble H. Richard Niebuhr's five models, which he introduced more than seventy years ago.[25] Hans Frei described five types of theology according to names of persons, with one in the nineteenth century and four in the twentieth—thus completely ignoring patristic, medieval, and early-modern Christian thinkers. The first three theologians that Frei mentioned are liberal (Gordon Kaufman, David Tracy, and Friedrich Schleiermacher); the fourth one is dogmatic (Karl Barth); and the fifth one is linguistic (D. Z. Phillips).[26] Since many scholars have criticized the constructing of models, I will not enter into an assessment of Bevans' or Niebuhr's or Frei's models. Nevertheless I think that their descriptions of the internal factors and of the models are instructive.

Lastly, from 1970 to this day, eclecticism has reigned in Catholic and Protestant churches.

---

23. Bevans, *Models of Contextual Theology*, 12–15.

24. Bevans, *Models of Contextual Theology*, 31–33 and 139–43.

25. See Niebuhr, *Christ and Culture*. Interestingly the idea of describing models can be traced to Ernst Troeltsch, that is, towards the beginning of the twentieth century; see Troeltsch, *The Social Teaching of the Christian Churches*.

26. See Frei, *Types of Christian Theology*, 28–55.

Methodologies in Systematic Theology

Concluding Remarks

This chapter retraced the main stages of Christian thinking over 2000 years. I emphasized the issue of how the Bible is received, described the practice of the patristic and of the monastic thinkers, analysed the mind and the method of the scholastics, presented the ways in which modern theologians coped with the intellectual challenges of their time, and finally insisted on the varieties of twentieth-century theologies.

In our next chapter, we shall engage in a more extended discussion bearing on the plurality of theologies and of the quests for truth.

2

Principles of Catholic Theology

Theology should be ecumenical. Not only Catholics, but also Orthodox and Protestants do accept, in practice and sometimes in principle, several of the principles that will be presented in this chapter. Theology is a collaborative endeavor, which requires mutual listening and respect for numerous approaches that are complementary or divergent, depending on which specific doctrine is studied.

A Plurality of Theologies

"One faith, several theologies," declared Popes John XXIII and Paul VI. In Augustine's, Thomas Aquinas's and Bernard Lonergan's epistemology, faith is the reception of *truths*, which operates on the level of judgment, whereas theology, which operates on the level of understanding (*fides quaerens intellectum*, "faith seeking understanding"), consists in explicating and systematically connecting the *meanings* of Christian beliefs.[1]

Obviously the truths remain the same, while we can say that the meanings do change to a certain extent. The meanings *do*

---

1. See Roy, *Engaging the Thought of Bernard Lonergan*, 92–101, and Index, at "intentionality, levels of," 238.

change since the objects of belief are understood differently according to various milieus (for example the differences between the four Gospels) and according to various epochs (for example the differences between patristic and scholastic styles of thinking). However meanings *do not* change insofar as they amount to church judgments; in this case, they have been identified in precise, universal and normative texts that assert definite meanings in their respective historical context.[2] So, while the Bible and the ecumenical councils are normative for systematic theologies, the latter have to be creative, given the evolution of cultures.

In fact, there is not *one* biblical theology because the Bible is pluralistic, although there are overlappings between biblical theologies. Likewise, in our twenty-first century each systematic theology takes into account the concerns and questions of its culture—and even of other cultures—and consequently elaborates its own perspective. Theologians have the duty to refer frequently to the word of God so as not to forget or undervalue some aspects of revelation. To achieve this goal, it is important to eschew the deviance of a self-sufficient reason, namely rationalism.[3]

Given those considerations, the status of biblical theology, also termed "salvation history," is problematic. Its beginning as an entity in itself can be traced to the Protestant Johann Philipp Gabler at the end of the eighteenth century. He distinguished between biblical and dogmatic theology. For him, biblical theology was simply an historical investigation into the successive beliefs of the biblical authors. However it had to precede dogmatic theology, which intended to be systematic. So the former is indispensable as a preliminary overal view of revelation held by biblical authors, while the latter must follow and, taking into account two millennia of Christian hermeneutics, must offer a systematic construction of revelation.[4]

---

2. See Neuner and Dupuis, eds., *The Christian Faith in the Doctrinal Documents of the Catholic Church*, Introduction to the First Edition.

3. For a contrast between a rationalistic philosophy of religion (Hegel's) and a philosophy of religion that is informed by Revelation (Thomas Aquinas's), see Heide, *Timeless Truth in the Hands of History*.

4. Hermeneutics will be explained in chapter 5.

In this respect, narrative theologies are in the same situation as biblical theologies. Over the last decades, narrative theologies have become popular, notably because of a dissatisfaction regarding the *abstractness* of several forms of systematic theology. The *concreteness* of narrative theologies makes them look closer to the religious experience of the readers whom they address. However most of the narrative theologians suffer from a Kantian bias, which asserts that religious affirmations are useful to the believers' motivations; hence they merely provide subjective meanings, and not truths.

Moreover the disparities between the various narrative theologies often amounts to incompatibilities and even to oppositions in terms of Christian doctrine. As a result no narrative theology can deal with this serious problem and, unless we opt for relativism, we need a function of systematic theology called "dialectic" in order to come to grips with this issue.[5] Nevertheless Edward Oakes correctly points out that "narrative was never ignored or denied in pre-Enlightenment theology, however propositions-ridden it might have seemed. But those particular Christian narratives (usually of the Bible, but also of saints' lives) were always assumed to be part of one all-encompassing narrative, within which 'propositional' theology did its work."[6] Furthermore Paul Griffiths helpfully characterizes the difference between narrative theology and systematic theology when he declares that the former is "indexed to a time" whereas the latter is not. Consequently only systematic theology has the potential to be in a sense timeless, namely universal.[7]

Insofar as styles of theology are concerned, we can think of the differences between Irenaeus (who died around 200) and Augustine (354–430). The former's thinking is rich and yet undifferentiated, whereas the latter's thinking is differentiated. For his

---

5. See Lonergan, *Method in Theology*, 220–49. We shall go back to that book in a subsequent chapter.

6. Oakes, "Apologetics and the Pathos of Narrative Theology," 38–39.

7. See Griffiths, "The Limits of Narrative Theology," 218, 220, 230, and 232. Readers will find in this piece a sound assessment of the pros and cons of narrative theology.

part, Irenaeus' theology is undifferentiatedly christocentric as he defends the unity of the person of the incarnate Son against the Gnostics. His principle of organization in *Against Heresies* has been characterized as the *oikonomía* of salvation. For Irenaeus, God's plan is realized in four main economies or types of covenant: with Noah, Abraham, Moses and Christ.[8]

By contrast, in *Teaching Christianity (De Doctrina Christiana)* Augustine begins by presenting God as Trinity and submits that love is the key to interpreting Holy Scripture.[9] Later in his life, in his *De Trinitate* he engages in a protracted theological reflection on who God is.[10] In particular, he sets apart two forms of consciousness in Christ: the divine and the human. He contends that there are in John's Gospel two categories of pronouncements: those in which Christ speaks as God and those in which he speaks as man. For example, Christ talks as only God can talk, as he says, "Before Abraham was, I Am" (Jn 8:58)[11]; Christ thus talks as the Lord did in Exodus 3:14. However, as a human being located in space and time and as subject to biological needs, he says, "I am thirsty" (Jn 19:28).

We can likewise think of the Greek Church Father Gregory of Nazianzen, who composed theological tracks as well as poems, of Thomas Aquinas, whose *Summa Theologiae* is very theoretical but whose eucharistic hymns were commissioned by the pope and introduced into the Catholic liturgy, of the German thinker Novalis, who wrote both poetry and essays, of John Henry Newman, who was a preacher, an essayist, a controversialist, a correspondent, and an author of poems, of the French Gabriel Marcel, who created plays for the theatre and also expressed himself through essays, and of others in the nineteenth and the twentieth century who did something similar.

---

8. Irenaeus, *Adversus Haereses*, Book III, chap. 11, no. 8.

9. See Augustine, *Teaching Christianity (De Doctrina Christiana)*. Our chapter 3 will detail his view of Christian teaching.

10. Augustine, *The Trinity*, Book I, chap. 2.

11. The "I Am" recurs in John: 6:20; 8:24, 28 & 58; 13:19; 18:5–6 & 8.

Principles of Catholic Theology

Traditions and Tradition

It is important to take into account the traditions, both in the Bible and in church history, which are embodied in communities. Underlying the traditions (in the plural) is a normative Tradition (in the singular).[12] Yet this Tradition is always articulated in a particular language, in a particular set of concepts namely in a conceptuality, hence in a particular line of thought that functions within a limited perspective, within a definite context, for example the intentions and statements of a biblical writer or of a council. If we take into consideration the concerns, questions and answers expressed in a specific environment (past or present), we shall not construe them as telling the *whole* truth on a topic. Whenever novel concerns and questions emerge, the Christian doctrines ought to be reformulated and re-presented thanks to the adoption of new approaches.

The Catholic theology that was elaborated during the modern era, mostly in Rome, is *only one* among the traditions worthy of examination. Its basic assumption is that over 2000 years Catholic teaching has always been the same, with minor differences. It is based on the illusion that it has always been the same from time immemorial and we can say, with Lonergan, that it is classicist, namely built on one, uniform culture. As a result it has not been able to meet head-on the challenge of the modern historical-mindedness. In contrast to the modern Catholic "dogmatic theology," twentieth- and twenty-first century theologies employ the historical method in the contextualized interpretations of texts, which must always be situated in their contexts.

Thus Lonergan rules out, for theology, a *classicist* notion according to which there would be only one culture, and teaches that we need an *empirical* notion of culture that earnestly takes into account the data of each particular culture. By doing so, he nevertheless avoids relativism. Hence these three positions:

---

12. See Congar, *Tradition and Traditions*. In chapter 8 we shall return to Congar's elucidation of this issue.

- Classicism = one culture, one theology
- Empirical mind = relativity and plurality of cultures = moderate pluralism
- Relativism = radical pluralism[13]

While rejecting relativism, it is helpful to acknowledge *relativity*, namely the awareness that any position is *relative to* an historical context. Therefore we need an ecumenical *plurality*, which rules out classicism as well as radical pluralism. In sum, what is to be commended is plurality, not pluralism (except if 'pluralism' is construed as plurality or moderate pluralism, which is often the case in Lonergan's works). This plurality includes symbolic as well as conceptual kinds of thinking.

Any particular tradition can convey universal truths, albeit always in keeping with its own perspective. Consequently students of religion have the task of comparing the perspectives, of discovering how much they overlap, and of how much they are open to the same reality. As soon as we start comparing perspectives, we are no longer enclosed in our own perspective. On the contrary our own perspective to a certain extent expands and changes.

Sources and the Hierarchy of Truth

To be normative, the Christian tradition must be faithful to biblical revelation, to ecumenical councils, and to the popes' infallible definitions (the Immaculate Conception of Mary in 1854 and the Assumption of Mary in 1950). The ecumenical councils—also called general or universal councils—and the solemn papal declarations regarding faith and morals constitute the *extraordinary magisterium*; they are *infallible* and thus binding for all Catholics. However, those infallible definitions are accompanied by non-infallible but supporting considerations. One can sometimes go beyond the letter of a council's text, but never go against the

---

13. On classicism and relativism, see Roy, *Engaging the Thought of Bernard Lonergan*, 102–17.

intention that impelled the assertion of a dogma by the extraordinary magisterium. The intention is found in the living situation of a council, with its issues and concerns.

The other pronouncements by the pope or by episcopal conferences constitute the *ordinary* magisterium and are *fallible*. Cardinal Josef Ratzinger introduced a novel category, which he called "definitive," which seemed to stand half-way between the infallible and the fallible exercise of the magisterium. Ratzinger argued that this third kind of teaching, for instance the problem of women's ordination to the priesthood, was strictly and intimately connected with revelation and therefore had to be firmly accepted and held. However, far from being helpful, this term "definitive" could be seen as a fallible teaching.

In the seventh century Pope Honorius I's *fallible* opinion that Christ possessed solely one will was condemned by the Third Council of Constantinople, which *infallibly* taught that he possessed two wills, a divine and a human will. So, after intense studies, competent experts have the duty to nuance, qualify or discard some declarations of the ordinary magisterium, which either turned out to be obsolete or were already erroneous. History informs us that past interdictions (for instance, the prohibition of lending with interests, the condemnation of Galileo's views in astronomy, the denial of religious freedom, the rejection of modern exegesis, or the repudiation of women's leadership in the Church) have been abandoned by Church authorities. These facts illustrate that other revisions will happen in the future, such as the diaconate or even the priesthood for women.

In the teaching of theological topics, there is a "hierarchy of truths."[14] Thus St. Thomas distinguishes between truths that "constitute the substance of faith" (*sunt per se substantia fidei*) and truths that "belong to faith only secondarily" (*non pertinent ad fidem nisi per accidens*).[15]

Second, the sources were called "theological topics" (*loci theologici*) by the Lutheran Melanchthon, and at approximately the

---

14. See Henn, "Hierarchy of Truths," 464–66.
15. Aquinas, *Scriptum super Libros Sententiarum*, Book II, d. 12, q. 1, a. 2.

same time by the Catholic Melchior Cano. We can interpret those theological topics for today and list them in an order of priority, as follows: the Bible, traditionally called the *norma non normata* (Latin for "the norm of norms that is not normed") (which is the germinal nucleus, from which all subsequent doctrines evolved), the ecumenical councils, the Catechism of the Catholic Church, the patristic writers, the local councils, the bishops' national conferences, the historians, the mystics, the doctors of the Church, the theologians, the philosophers, the sages of the non-Christian religions, the specialists in the religious studies or in the human sciences (for instance psychology and sociology of religion), etc.

Theology is done with the light of faith, assisted by reason. However, like philosophy of religion, religious studies (for example psychology and sociology of religion) are done by reason alone. Still, the latter are very useful as mines of information and of discernment.

Systematic Theology and Biblical Texts

The treatise on God must begin with the Bible, since it is divine revelation. However we must avoid biblicism, that is, simply repeating what the Bible tells us. We must interpret divine revelation for our culture for three reasons.

First, our mental categories are not the same as those of the ancient Jews; consequently we have to translate the biblical message into our categories. This process of inculturation is what the Church has done for twenty centuries. Just think of the difference between the New Testament and the early councils, or the Greek or Latin Fathers, or the medieval doctors, or the modern Catholic theologies in the wake of the Protestant Reformation, or the response to the challenge of the Enlightenment.

The second reason is that the Bible does not offer us an organized doctrine on God. We find in it narratives and metaphorical statements even in the New Testament that, far from always being consistent, are often contradictory. For instance, God is said to forgive and yet he gets angry and he punishes the sins of the parents by turning not only against them but even against their children and grandchildren. Furthermore he repents about his previous decisions and changes his mind, so that over the centuries many believers have not been quite sure about his fidelity.

The third reason is that in a scientific age human curiosity raises what the Canadian Jesuit Bernard Lonergan called "questions for systematics." They are questions that, in order to be answered, require an explicit overall view of the subject matter. Such is the case for chemistry with its periodic table. Such is also the case for theology with Thomas Aquinas's *Summa Theologiae*. Still, because we are not medievals, we ask questions that he did not pose and therefore we need a systematic theology for our time, which integrates his insights while going beyond them on certain points.

Philosophy's Role within Theology

The influential, Protestant church historian Adolf von Harnack (1851–1930) denounced what he dubbed "the hellenization of Christianity" carried out by the patristic church. In his opinion, this process consisted in adopting Hellenic way of thinking that replaced the biblical God with a Greek god.[16] The living God of faith became, in church theology and teaching, the abstract god of reason. The compassionate, suffering with us, interacting with us, God revealed in Jesus Christ, was supplanted by the impassible, immutable, remote god of the philosophers.

Although I disagree, this thesis nevertheless contains more than a grain of truth. On the one hand, it is true that the god of Plato, Aristotle and Plotinus is approached intellectually—from the perspective of the unity of all things, as the source of this unity. Moreover he is conceived as self-sufficient, unconcerned with what happens to human beings, and thus very different from the biblical God who enters into an interpersonal relationship with his beloved people and gives us his only beloved Son.

---

16. On this issue see Lonergan, *A Second Collection*, 11–30.

On the other hand, had Christian theology excluded the assistance of Greek concepts and distinctions, the Church of the first five centuries would not have been capable of clarifying vital beliefs concerning the Trinity and the person of Jesus Christ. Without Greek philosophy, Augustine would not have thought out the relations of time and eternity, and Thomas Aquinas would not have understood and employed the all-important distinction between existence and essence, which he borrowed from the Muslim thinker Avicenna. (According to Pierre Hadot, the distinction was originally coined by Porphyry, the first disciple of Plotinus.) In a word, had Greek logic and metaphysics been ignored, Christian theology would have looked childish and would have been discredited.

Beginning with Tertullian (ca. 160–ca. 230), countless Christian writers deprecated the intrusion of philosophy into theology, an intrusion that presumably corrupted it. But it is not philosophy as such that is detrimental to theology, but *bad* philosophy. For example, the voluntarism of late-medieval nominalism, which portrayed God as having an absolute power that could do anything not intrinsically contradictory—an absolute power that seems to be irrational, incomprehensible, and arbitrary. By contrast, Aquinas's philosophy envisions divine power as wise, coherent, and communicable to believers, who have a modest share in it. Likewise we observe defects in Scotus's conceptualism, in seventeenth-century rationalism, in eighteenth-century deism, Kantianism, Hegelianism, etc.

In fact, even those who rail against philosophy—for instance Luther, Calvin and Pascal—unwittingly and disastrously use late-medieval nominalism, in the case of those I have just mentioned. As a matter of fact the choice is not between having philosophy or no philosophy within theology, but rather between having good or bad philosophy within theology.[17] This requires that theologians *critically* adopt philosophical ideas and approaches. Thomas

---

17. On this issue, see Lonergan, "Christology Today," 74: "Contemporary Catholic theology [in the early 1970s] deprecates any intrusion from philosophy. The result inevitably is, not no philosophy, but unconscious philosophy, and only too easily bad philosophy."

Guarino calls this process "purifying philosophy" and he indicates that great minds such as Origen, the Cappadocian Fathers, Augustine and Aquinas, while borrowing concepts from the philosophers, managed to clarify and re-express Christian thought for their epoch.[18] So theology can be simultaneously inculturated and countercultural.

Concluding Remarks

This chapter delved into thorny problems such as the plurality of theologies and the sources of truth. The basic distinction between meaning and truth, and between the several traditions and the one Tradition were emphasized. Much scholarship is needed to understand how the Tradition emerges from particular traditions. Methodological clarity about such issues demands the intellectual flexibility that a correct historical consciousness can provide.

18. Guarino, *Foundations of Systematic Theology*, 56–58.

3

Augustine of Hippo

Saint Augustine was a teacher of rhetoric in the late Roman Empire. He converted to Christianity at the age of 32 and subsequently was made bishop of Hippo, in Roman North Africa. He engendered an extraordinary way of understanding both the Bible and Christian existence. It is not an exaggerated statement to assert that prior to the twentieth-century hermeneutics, Augustine's conception of interpretation was the most influential view in Western theology and philosophy.[1]

This chapter is divided into two sections: first, the *objective* aspect of Augustine's methodology, consisting of a continuous reading of the Bible and a borrowing from Neoplatonism, and second, the *subjective* aspect, that is, the human person's requirements for correctly interpreting one's existence.

The Objective Aspect of his Methodology

The meditation of the Bible and the recourse to the Christian creed constitute the objective grounding of his methodology.

---

1. See Grondin, *Introduction to Philosophical Hermeneutics*, xiii–xiv, 32–39, 46, and 119.

Augustine of Hippo

In a very long volume Isabelle Bochet detailed the numerous elements of Augustine's hermeneutic and she asserts that "the Augustinian hermeneutic is first of all a Scriptural hermeneutic."[2] Regarding this hermeneutic let us retrace his evolution. Before he became a Christian, his interest in Neoplatonic philosophy prevented him from making sense of several biblical texts. As he himself avowed, his philosophical knowledge puffed him up. Meanwhile, Ambrose, bishop of Milan, in his sermons helped him to see that many passages of Holy Scripture make sense, provided that one has recourse to allegory as an interpretive tool. He then realized that the biblical narratives often have a symbolic value for human thinking.[3]

At the very beginning of his *Teaching Christianity* he offers us guidelines for correctly construing the Bible:

> There are some rules for dealing with the scriptures, which I consider can be not inappropriately passed on to students, enabling them to make progress not only by reading others who have opened up the hidden secrets of the divine literature, but also by themselves opening them up to yet others again.[4]

In fact, the purpose of his writing is to help Christian teachers to take advantage of Bible-reading so as to grow and to make others grow in the love for God.

In book 1, no. 2, he justifies his method by having recourse to the difference between realities, signs, and words.[5] The latter are employed in order to refer to realities. He mentions "wood, a

2. Bochet, "*Le firmament de l'Écriture*," 11; see 501.

3. St. Paul had recourse to allegories as he construed Old Testament texts, for instance in Gal 4:21–31, where he instructively used an "allegory" (*allēgoroúmena*, verse 24). However, as is well known, Augustine often indulged in farfetched allegories.

4. Augustine, *Teaching Christianity*, Prologue, no. 1. Further references to this work will be given in my text. Please note that the Latin word *doctrina* is correctly translated here by "teaching," because it implies a definite learning on the part of Augustine's readers.

5. I have departed from Hill's translation by rendering the Latin *res* by "realities" instead of by "things," so as to include persons among the *res*.

stone, an animal" as examples of realities; however, realities themselves can also refer to other realities. As a result, both words and realities are often signs pointing to something else. Realities that indicate other realities are the basis of metaphorical meanings.

In book 3, Augustine warns his readers "to beware of taking a figurative expression literally"; for example, "sabbath" designates more than a day of the week and "sacrifice" designates more than a physical immolation (no. 9). He states that some words, such as "the wrath of God" (in Rom 2:5) and "have crucified [their flesh]" (in Gal 5:24) are "metaphorical," alias "figurative" (nos. 17 and 24).[6] But "If it [a sentence] is an expression of command, either forbidding infamy or crime, or ordering usefulness or kindness, it is not figurative" (no. 24).

Moreover, he asks his readers to take account of the contexts in which words appear. "We should not think it is *de rigueur* for us to assume that a thing always has to signify what it happens to signify in one passage by its resemblance to something else." He gives as an example the word "yeast" in Mt 16:6 and in Lk 13:21 (no. 35). A bit further on, he asserts: "In the same way there are other things which, considered not in their general use, but in any particular instance, signify not only two different things but sometimes even several, depending on the place the sentence occurs in" (no. 37).

Earlier in *Teaching Christianity* he draws attention to his experience of enjoying obscure comparisons (namely metaphors) such as in the Songs of Songs 4:2 (book 2, no. 7), because "discovering things is much more gratifying if there has been some difficulty in the search for them" (book 2, no. 8; see also book 4, no. 15).

Still in book 2, he realistically recommends that learners should start with topics in our sacred writings that are less obscure:

> Those things that are put clearly in them [the sacred writings] . . . are to be studied with the utmost care and diligence. . . . Only then, however, after acquiring some familiarity with the actual style of the divine scriptures,

---

6. In sermon 89, nos. 4–6, Augustine equates "the proper sense" with "the literal sense," and "the symbolic sense" with "the figurative sense." See *Sermons III/3 (51–94)*.

should one proceed to try to open up and unravel their obscurities, in such a way that instances from the plainer passages are used to cast light on the more obscure utterances (no. 14).

Likewise, in a sermon he states: "Actually in the whole wide field of the holy scriptures we are nourished by the passages that are clear, exercised by those that are obscure; the first kind relieve us from hunger, the second save us from boredom."[7]

In "The Advantage of Believing" Augustine writes: "The whole of the scripture that we call the Old Testament is offered to those who seriously wish to understand it under four aspects: as history, as explanation, as analogy, and as allegory." He explains:

> Accordingly, there is the aspect of history, when we are taught what was written or what happened, of what did not happen but was written only as a story. There is the aspect of explanation, when we are shown the reasons why something was said or done. There is the aspect of analogy, when we are shown how the two testaments, le Old and the New, do not contradict each other. There is the aspect of allegory, when we are taught that what was written is not to be taken literally but has to be understood in a figurative sense.[8]

He adds, "Our Lord Jesus Christ and the apostles used all these methods."[9]

However, as indicated by the French historian Henri-Irénée Marrou, Augustine included history in his method: Judaic, Roman, and Christian history.[10] This point is important, given the significance of modern history for modern Christians. Furthermore Marrou pointed out that Augustine uses logic in extracting various propositions from the Bible, the Church councils, and the previous

---

7. Sermon 71, no. 11, in *Sermons III/3 (51–94)*.
8. Augustine, "The Advantage of Believing," no. 5.
9. "The Advantage of Believing," no. 6; see nos. 6–8.
10. See Marrou, *Saint Augustin et la fin de la culture antique*, 417–22 and 463–67.

patristic writers; he also employs dialectic in his controversies, thus anticipating, to a certain extent, the scholastic method.[11]

The second objective source of correct interpretation is the Christian creed. In various studies, Augustine states and details the Christian creed as the "rule of faith" (*regula fidei*), namely as the foundation of Catholic interpretation.

In sermon 213 he speaks of a symbol (*symbolum*) as a reminder of the catechumens' faith and he defined it as "a briefly compiles rule of faith, intended to instruct the mind without overburdening the memory; to be said in a few words, from which much is to be gained."[12] In sermon 212 he explained that "everything that you are going to hear in the symbol is already contained in the divine documents of the holy scriptures." He adds:

> The God who has called you to his kingdom and his glory will ensure that it is also written on your hearts by the Holy Spirit, once you have been born again by his grace; so that you may love what you believe, and faith may work in you through love.[13]

In terms of pedagogy, he distinguishes between the apprenticeship of the well-educated and the apprenticeship of the unlearned. He insisted on the need for teachers to be humble:

> When, therefore, these persons who seem to surpass all other people in the art of speaking, come to be made Christians, we ought to convey to them more fully than to the illiterate an earnest warning to clothe themselves in Christian humility, and learn not to despise those whom they know as shunning more carefully faults of character than faults of diction, and also that they should not even presume to compare with a pure heart the trained tongue which they had been wont even to prefer.[14]

---

11. *Saint Augustin et la fin de la culture antique*, 458–63.

12. Saint Augustine, sermon 213, no. 2, in *Sermons III/6*; see sermon 214, no. 1, and sermon 398, no. 1, in *Sermons III/10*.

13. Sermon 212, no. 2, in *Sermons III/6*.

14. Augustine, *The First Catechetical Instruction*, chap. 9, 13; I have made that translation more inclusive.

Augustine of Hippo

We shall see, in the rest of this chapter, that Augustine always closely links in his methodological advice human reason with subjective factors, such as humility, piety, faith, hope, and love, namely, as in this quotation, "a pure heart."

Subjective Aspects of His Methodology

Intellectual curiosity is the first subjective component of his methodology. He urges us in these terms: "Let us seek the one who is to be found; let us seek the one who has been found. In order for one who must be found to be sought, he must be hidden. In order for one who has been found to be sought, he must be beyond measure."[15] Or, in a more succinct rendering: "Let us seek as people who are going to find, and let us find as people who are going to continue seeking."[16] Augustine surely is one of the greatest models for seekers, along with Socrates, Thomas Aquinas, and all great philosophers and theologians.

The second subjective component is Augustine's keenness to attain truth. Owing to his discovery of Neoplatonism, which he reports in his *Confessions*, his rejection of Manichaeism led to the second aspect of his methodology. There he avows that at first he entertained false ideas about God and evil.[17] Later, as he read the writings of the Platonists, particularly Cicero's work *Hortensius*, Augustine underwent an intellectual conversion and acquired correct ideas about God and evil.[18] So, what is important methodologically is the dialectical character of his controversies, against the Manichaeans, the Donatists, and the Pelagians.

15. Augustine, Homily 63, no.1, in *Homilies on the Gospel of John*.

16. Augustine, *The Trinity*, book IX, chap. 1; I have slightly reworked Hill's translation. See equally book XV, Prologue, chap. 2: "So great a good . . . is sought in order to be found all the more delightfully, and it is found in order to be sought all the more avidly."

17. Augustine, *The Confessions*, book III, chap. 3 (6), book IV, chaps. 28–31 (16), and book V, chap. 10 (18–20).

18. *The Confessions*, book I, chap. 2 (2–4), and book III, chap. 4 (7). See the entire book VII. I will go back to Augustine's thoughts on evil in a subsequent writing.

Personal wisdom is the third subjective component of his methodology. In a discussion about the order of the universe, he agrees with one of his interlocutors who holds that "The sage is united with God, for he knows himself. This results at once from the definition that you have given me, namely that the one who knows God is united with God, and from what we said, namely that what the sage knows is united with God."[19]

Evidently, for Augustine the sage is the person who has found where wisdom can be found, namely in the contemplation of both the eternal God and the temporal realities. The first kind of contemplation bears on the eternal, whereas the second kind bears on the rather restricted temporal. So Augustine strongly contrast the two objects of contemplation, which he calls "things divine" (*res divinae*) and "things human (*res humanae*). Therefore he firmly suggests that we ought to properly call "wisdom" (*sapientia*) knowledge of the divine realities, and properly call "knowledge" (*scientia*) knowledge of the human realities.

He nonetheless correlates this twofold experience by stating that the participation in the temporal "is equally valuable for gaining these eternal realities, and finally that the very virtues by which one lives sagaciously, courageously, moderately, and justly in this time of mortality must be related to this faith which though temporal itself leads to eternity."[20]

In one of his sermons, he delineates an analogy between our knowledge of our own soul and our knowledge of God. To an opponent whose god [small g, sic] is a mere visible idol, Augustine replies by drawing attention to the existence of the human soul:

> You asked where God [Augustine's God] is, while I ask where my questioner himself is. . . . I am inquiring about my questioner; I can see his face, see his body, hear his voice, take a look at his tongue; I'm inquiring about the one who turns his eyes to me, who wags his tongue, who utters his voice, who asks questions because he wants

---

19. Augustine, *De ordine*, book II, section 2, no. 5.
20. *The Trinity*, book 14, no. 3.

Augustine of Hippo

to know the answers. The sum total of what I'm talking about is the soul.[21]

Of course Augustine is fully aware of the fact that religious language, while inadequate, is nevertheless valid because it is analogical.[22] Let us see how he describes this analogical character:

> You say, 'Show me your God'; I say, 'Show me your spirit.... Your spirit is invisible. And yet it is in you, better than your body; while my God is better than your spirit. So how am I to show you my God, when you can't show me your spirit, and I can show you that my God is better than your spirit.

Augustine then demonstrates that as we can know our own spirit indirectly through its works, we can also know God indirectly through his works in the universe. And he concludes that section 4 of his sermon as follows, "The whole of that, which you marvel at in yourself—the one who made that, that's who my God is."[23]

In another sermon, Augustine underscores the usefulness of analogical language regarding the emergence of the eternal Word in God: "Not even I who am speaking to you, not even I understand. But thinking about these things makes us stretch ourselves, stretching ourselves expands us, expansion increases our capacity. Not even with increased capacity will we be able to understand the whole of it." He then proceeds to further explain what the inner word is in our minds:

> When I was thinking about what I was going to say to you, there was already a word in my mind. I mean, I wouldn't be saying it to you unless I had thought of it first. I found you were Latin speaking, so a Latin word had to be offered you; while if you had been Greek, I would have had to speak to you in Greek, and present you with a Greek word. That word in my mind is neither

---

21. Sermon 223A, no. 4, in Augustine, *Sermons III/6*.

22. On the partial inadequacy of our language, see Roy, *God: Polarities in Language*, forthcoming, chapter 10, section titled "Inadequate and nonetheless Valid Representations."

23. Sermon 223A, no. 4.

Latin nor Greek; what's in my mind altogether precedes these languages.[24]

To appreciate better Augustine's thought on how to interpret the Christian heritage, we must take account of his view of love, which is the last and most important subjective attitude that is needed. In a homily, he urges his auditors:

> Let us not love the world, not the realities that are in the world.... All these realities are good, but woe to you if you love created realities and abandon the creator.... As long as they use created realities not temperately but inordinately, the creator is disdained.

And he proposes a comparison:

> Brothers, if a bridegroom made a ring for his bride, and she loved the ring that she had received more than her bridegroom, who made the ring, in the same way wouldn't an adulterous soul be detected in the bridegroom's very gift, even though she loved what the bridegroom gave her?[25]

To know more about love, we must return to book 1 of *De Doctrina Christiana*. At no. 3, Augustine subdivides realities into those that it is appropriate to enjoy (*frui*) and those that it is appropriate to use (*uti*). At no. 4, he defines them as follows: "Enjoyment . . . consists in clinging to something lovingly for its own sake, while use consists in referring what has come your way to what your love aims at obtaining, provided, that is, it deserves to be loved." If Augustine identifies God as the highest Being, he nevertheless does not disparage God's creation; "to use" is not instrumentally reduced to a sort of tool. He also declares that we must "proceed from temporal and bodily realities to grasp those that are eternal and spiritual." At no. 5, he infers: "The realities therefore that are to be enjoyed are the Father and the Son and the Holy Spirit, in fact the Trinity, one supreme reality, and one which is shared in common by all who enjoy it."

---

24. Reference lost.
25. Reference lost.

At no. 21, he asserts that "none of us ought either to find enjoyment in ourselves, if you consider the matter straightforwardly, because we ought not either to love ourselves for our own sakes, but for the sake of the one [God] whom we are to enjoy." Therefore love of self is good provided it is related to love for God. The same applies to love for our neighbors: "So if you ought not to love yourself for your own sake, but for the sake of the one to whom your love is most rightly directed as its end, other people must not take offense if you also love them for God's sake and not their own." And he draws the inference: "So all who love their neighbors in the right way ought so to deal with them that they too love God with all their heart, all their soul, all their mind."[26]

At no. 27, he adds a corollary: "But when it [the Bible] says, *You shall love your neighbor as yourself*, love of yourself by yourself is being simultaneously included." At no. 29, he writes:

> The consequence of this is that we should love our enemies; after all, we have nothing to fear from them, because they cannot possibly deprive us of what we love; instead we feel sorry for them, because the more they hate us, the more it shows how far they are cut off from the one whom we love.

And he adjoins a note of hope: "If, however, they are converted and turn back to him, they must needs love both him as their bliss-conferring good, and us as their companions in enjoying such an unimaginable good."

At this point, one may wonder about the significance of Augustine's long excursus on love in the *De Doctrina Christiana*. It is because, for him, love of God and neighbor is the sum of what Holy Scripture teaches, and because, by living out such love, one is enabled to find the basic meaning of Holy Scripture. "So if it seems to you that you have understood the divine scriptures, or any part of them, in such a way that by this understanding you do not build up this twin love of God and neighbor, then you have not yet understood them" (no. 40).

---

26. On the various kinds of love and their mutual relations, see Roy, *Self-Actualization and the Radical Gospel*, chaps. 3 and 6.

Methodologies in Systematic Theology

Concluding Remarks

Augustine's profundity is expressed by a remark he made early in his life, at the end of a discussion with friends: "Experience shows that when people of little moment apply themselves to great matters, these matters lend greatness to them."[27]

I will conclude with a final quotation from Augustine:

> If you cannot restrain the eagerness with which you were persuaded to arrive at truth by reason (*ratio*), then you must be prepared to tread many long roundabout ways, in order to accept as guide only the reason that deserves that name, namely the *true* reason; and not only the true reason, but the reason that is *certain*, and a reason that is so much a total stranger to any mendacious falsity (inasmuch as it [truth] is discoverable at all by the human person) that no false or specious arguments might misguide you away from it.

Augustine's interlocutor replied, "May reason guide me and lead me the way it wants, provided it be to the goal!" And Augustine retorted, "God will give you this—he who with regard to such matters alone [namely the pursuits of religious truth], or certainly with regard to these, should be implored."[28]

---

27. Augustine, *Against the Academics*, book 1, chap. 2, no. 6; translation slightly modified to make it inclusive.

28. Augustine, *The Greatness of the Soul*, chap. 7 no. 12. I would prefer translating *quantitas* by "size" or "measure."

4

Albert the Great and Thomas Aquinas

Because the German Albert and the Italian Thomas share the traits of medieval scholasticism expounded in chapter 1, we shall not repeat those traits here. Since scholars recognize that Thomas perfected Albert's thought, consequently this chapter will treat of Thomas more at length than of Albert. Their striking common enterprise intensified the integration of non-Christian philosophy into Catholic theology so as to provide an overal framework of thinking, namely an architectonic one.

Albert the Great, the First Medieval Aristotelian

The thirteenth-century scholar Albert the Great (around 1200–1280) was very interested in virtually all the disciplines of his time: theology, philosophy, mathematics, and the natural sciences, especially biology and botany. Consequently he was dubbed the *doctor universalis* and, given his very long life, his output became enormous. In particular, he was instrumental in having the

39

Methodologies in Systematic Theology

Dominicans, namely the Order of Preachers, to which he belonged, officially ratify the importance of philosophy in their formation.[1]

Even though thinkers like Boethius and Abelard had discussed Aristotle's logic (see chapter 1), Albert initiated a paraphrasing of Aristotle's writings. His conviction that the Greek Aristotle, "the philosopher," had much to offer to medieval philosophizing exemplifies the comparative method. Hence his interest not only in Aristotle, but also, for example, in the Neoplatonic author of the *Book of Causes*, in the Muslim Averroes, called "the Commentator," and in the Byzantine Dionysios the pseudo-Areopagite.[2] By examining ideas expressed by many non-Christian authors, he ranks as a model of ecumenical commitment.[3]

Albert's scholastic penchant is noticeable throughout his main commentary on Dionysios as he tries to systematize the often fragmentary thoughts offered by this Byzantine mystic.[4] Evidently, in the course of this recasting of Dionysios' vision, much of the imaginative and rhetorical forcefulness of the original work is lost. However another kind of beauty is gained: the luminosity of clear definitions systematically correlated in an overall metaphysical synthesis. Accordingly Albert tackled difficulties of interpreting particular texts of Dionysios and at times he was concerned about the adequacy of the two translations he was using.

Albert's commentary on Dionysios did not purport to replace the original religious experience of hearing the word of God in a liturgical setting, of interpreting it in a symbolic context, of appreciating the literary suggestiveness of Dionysios' writings, and of being challenged by their profundity. In his desire to know, Albert

---

1. Nonetheless Albert never could take this ratification for granted; see Tugwell, *Albert & Thomas*, 15 and 34–35.

2. I call him Dionysios, not Dionysius, because he was a Greek, not a Latin.

3. On Albert the Great, see Roy, "Medieval Latin Scholasticism: Some Comparative Features," 26–31.

4. For an English translation of Albert's commentary on Dionysios, see Tugwell, *Albert & Thomas*. Written though it was written in the 1980s, his Introduction to Albert in this volume still is the best available in the English-speaking world.

Albert the Great and Thomas Aquinas

raised questions which required for their answers the epistemological and metaphysical conceptuality he was patiently working out in a dialogue between Christian doctrine and views expressed by Aristotle, Neoplatonism, and Arabic philosophy.

Even though Albert was a scholastic, as a medieval—not modern—doctor he was fond of reading and commenting on the Bible, and his spirituality was shaped by the reading of the words of God with the assistance of the Holy Spirit. He wrote:

> Anyone who lacks the consolation of the Spirit falters spiritually through thirst and hunger; the body needs food if it is to stand firm in the battle, and it is the same with the spirit: unless it is fed with the word of God and with God's sweetness (*dulcedo*), it will inevitably abandon his work, power will fall from its hands. So we need often to be nourish by the sweetness of the word of God.[5]

Albert united prayer with thinking. As Tugwell wrote, "It is not difficult to accept the story that Albert used to declare that he often obtained by prayer the understanding of something that he could not master by study. What same Christian intellectual would say otherwise?"[6]

Moreover his spiritual sense extended to his attitude towards all members of any Christian group:

> If you want to be in unity with everyone, you should make your heart like your neighbor's heart, so that when he is happy, you are happy, and you grieve with him when he is grieving. But some people are like stones that have so many rough edges that they cannot possibly be put together with other stones to make a wall; wherever you put them their awkward shape immediately pushes out other stones. There is no way they can be joined together. Similarly if my heart is in distress and you are happy,

---

5. Albert, Commentary on Dionysios' fifth letter, an excerpt translated by Tugwell, *Albert & Thomas*, 30. I have replaced Tugwell's rendering of *dulcedo* from "charm" to "sweetness."

6. Peter of Prussia, *Legenda Alberti Magni*, translated in Tugwell, *Albert & Thomas*, 37.

your happiness sticks into me like an ill-shaped stone, so that our feelings cannot possibly come together.[7]

Thomas Aquinas, the Great Synthesizer

Albert's greatest disciple, Thomas Aquinas (1224/25–1274) was dubbed the *doctor angelicus*, probably for two reasons: because he was very pure, as his confessor testified after his death, and because, like angels, who always understand, without the mediation of the senses and the imagination, he quickly found answers to the questions that were continually popping up in his mind.

Thomas furthered and bettered his mentor's enterprise. His contribution consisted in his integrative power, which enabled him to organize the enormous material he inherited from his predecessors. As a matter of fact, when Thomas began teaching, virtually all the elements of his thought were there in his predecessors' writings. It is his synthesis of those elements that is typical of its genius.

Thomas integrated faith and reason. For instance he went beyond St. Paul's paradoxes as he commented on the famous first chapter of the apostle's First Letter to the Corinthians. With the aid of an effective distinction, namely to be against and to go beyond, he construed the "foolishness of the cross," which Paul had proclaimed, as being not *against* human reason but *beyond* reason's capacity to grasp it fully.[8] In Thomas's writings, one can observe a genuine attempt to find a glimpse of the truth in any objection, because there is always a sense in which the objector is right (to the extent that the objection may convey a resistance to some caricature of truth). Thanks to his listening disposition towards non-Christian sources, Thomas was able to resist the temptation of proving them wrong too expeditiously.

---

7. Albert, Commentary of John's Gospel, translated in Tugwell, *Albert & Thomas*, 36.

8. Aquinas, "Super Primam Epistolam ad Corinthios Lectura," Caput I, lectio 3.

This listening disposition was later reiterated by Ignatius of Loyola, as noted by a Thomist-Lonerganian scholar, who explained his own version of hermeneutics as follows:

> This is our attempt to be faithful to the Ignatian *praesupponendum*, which asks us to be more ready to put a good interpretation on another's statement than to condemn it as false (Ignatius Loyola, *Spiritual Exercises*, no. 22). But when a theologian moves from the positive thrust of his or her proposal to the negative criticism of earlier theologians who "got it wrong," we will often be critical precisely because the author himself or herself appears to set aside the *praesupponendum*.[9]

Moreover Thomas was aware that no sound theologizing is possible without a series of personal dispositions granted by God: (1) the supernatural virtues of faith, hope and charity, which establish a living relationship between God and the believers; (2) the infused cardinal virtues of prudence, fortitude, temperance and justice; and (3) the seven gifts of the Holy Spirit, which are wisdom, understanding, knowledge, counsel, piety, fortitude and fear.[10] Among these, two are more important than the other for our interest in his theological method: science (*scientia*) enables believers to elicit correct *judgments* about which *creaturely* realities are to be believed, whereas wisdom (*sapientia*) enables them to elicit correct *judgments* about the *divine* realities, out of the very experience of those realities.[11]

For Thomas the contrast between those two gifts is less stark than for Augustine (see our preceding chapter, on Augustine). In a fine contribution on that topic, Andreas Speer pointed out that because of his use of Aristotelian thought regarding the intellectual virtues of wisdom, understanding, and science, Thomas did not refer to Augustine, but to Aristotle as he treated of wisdom. Basing himself on Thomas's first writing, Speer explained:

---

9. Jean-Marc Laporte, *God One and Triune*, 141, footnote 3.
10. See Aquinas, *Summa Theologiae*, I–II, q. 68. See also Aquinas, *The Gifts of the Spirit*.
11. See Aquinas, *Summa Theologiae*, II–II, q. 9 and q. 45.

Methodologies in Systematic Theology

> Wisdom is defined as a certain eminent sufficiency in knowing, bearing in itself a certitude regarding great and extraordinary things, which are unknown to the others [who do not possess this wisdom]. This eminent sufficiency which occurs by a certain affinity to the divine and must be understood as a "virtus intellectualis" acquired "per studium et doctrinam," and which is inclined to the "intellectus principiorum," leads to the ability of judging all things.[12]

Here is how Marie-Dominique Chenu situated the role of those gifts:

> The gifts are perfections of the person superior to the virtues. The virtues ready us to respond to the moving power of reason in both interior and exterior acts. However, in order to be responsive to God's impulse in our lives, we need superior dispositions of readiness. These are called gifts, not only because they are infused (given freely) by God, but also because they render us quickly responsive to God's inspiration. . . . There must further be the prompting and moving power of the Holy Spirit.[13]

This is to say: the virtues are habits whose influence is rather constant and therefore general, whereas the gifts are punctual, therefore particular.

Aquinas distinguished *studiositas* (studiousness) and *curiositas* (curiosity). The former, a devotion to learning, is a virtue which sets the desire to know in the right direction. The latter, intemperate curiosity, is a multi-faceted disorder. Among its deviations listed by Thomas, two are most noteworthy. The first deviation is noticeable "when people are withdrawn by a less profitable study from a study that is an obligation incumbent on them." Second deviation is noticeable "when a person desires to know the truth

---

12. Speer, "Contemplation and Philosophy," 86. Speer is paraphrasing Aquinas, *Scriptum super Libros Sententiarum*, I, d. 35, a. 1. The « affinity to the divine » corresponds to Aquinas's *pati divina*, who quoted Dionysios' famous *pathein to theia*.

13. Chenu, *Aquinas and His Role in Theology*, 57 and 58; on Thomas as a "Master in Sacred Theology," see 15–33.

Albert the Great and Thomas Aquinas

about creatures without referring its knowledge to its due end, namely, the knowledge of God."[14]

Aquinas nevertheless saw intellectual pleasure as sustaining a deeper concern: attentiveness to the realities themselves that we know and love, beginning with God.

> Contemplation can be enjoyable (*delectabilis*) in two ways. First by virtue of the activity itself, because people delight in the activity which befits them according to their own nature or habit.... Secondly, contemplation may be delightful on the part of its object, insofar as one contemplates that which one loves.... There is delight in the contemplative life, not only by reason of the contemplation itself, but also by reason of the divine love.[15]

In his commentary on Matthew's Gospel, Aquinas remarked that "some hear that they may know, and these build upon understanding, and this is the building upon sand.... Hence, they build upon what is changeable. And some hear that they may do and love, and these build upon a rock, because they build upon what is firm and stable."[16] He continued, "But here it can be asked why the foundation which is in understanding is unstable, and is not firm, while that which is in emotion is." He answered:

> The reason is that understanding is of universals, for one cannot know many things except in the universal; this is why, wandering around the universal, there is no stability. But operations and emotions concern particulars, and the habitual good; so if temptation comes, one clings to that which is customary, namely to good works, and so one resists.[17]

Thomas said that the role of the teacher is to produce in the student that movement of mind by which he himself arrived at the truth:

14. Aquinas, *Summa Theologiae*, II–II, q. 167, a. 1; see q. 166.

15. Aquinas, *Summa Theologiae*, II–II, q. 180, a. 7.

16. Aquinas, *Commentary on the Gospel of Matthew*, chap. 7, lecture 2, no. 674.

17. Aquinas, *Commentary on the Gospel of Matthew*, no. 675.

> One person is said to teach another inasmuch as, by signs, he manifests to that other the reasoning process which he himself goes through by his own natural reason. And thus, through the instrumentality, as it were, of what is told him, the natural reason of the pupil arrives at a knowledge of the thing which he did not know.[18]

Elsewhere he pointed out the following pedagogical principle:

> Since there is a twofold way of acquiring knowledge—by discovery and by being taught –, the way of discovery is the higher, and the way of being taught is secondary. Thus it is said (in Aristotle's Nicomachean Ethics, I, 4): 'he indeed is the best who knows everything by himself; yet he is good who obeys the person who speaks aright.'[19]

Either one understand everything for oneself, or one is passively docile in the presence of a teacher. Of course one begins by receiving information and vocabulary; nevertheless it is more fruitful to try and think for oneself. This pursuit necessitates a dynamic openness to questions that are raised and to objections that arise concerning any theological position. Thus, taking questions seriously produces a stepping back vis-à-vis answers, hence a disquieting incertitude. It is profitable to accept this incertitude, because it allows students to enter into an indispensable stage, which leads to insights. Otherwise one does not learn to think critically and to help others think critically. As Aquinas wrote, "God so governs beings that he makes some of them to be causes of others in government, as a master who not only imparts knowledge to his disciples, but gives also the ability to teach others."[20]

Let us note that questioning does not regard the contents of *faith*, but the interpretations of faith that *theology* offers. As we shall see later in chapter 7, Bernard Lonergan distinguished, in Aquinas's theological method, between the establishment of doctrines and systematization:

---

18. Aquinas, *Disputed Questions on Truth*, q. 11, a. 1.
19. Aquinas, *Summa Theologiae*, III, q. 9, a. 4, ad 1.
20. Aquinas, *Summa Theologiae*, I, q. 103, a. 6.

Albert the Great and Thomas Aquinas

The classic example of this distinction between doctrines and systematics is provided by the fourth book of Aquinas's *Summa contra Gentiles*. There chapters 2 to 9 are concerned with the existence of God the Son, chapters 13 to 18 with the existence of the Holy spirit, chapters 27 to 39 with the existence of the Incarnation. But chapters 10 to 14 center in the question of the manner in which a divine generation is to be conceived. Similarly, chapters 10 to 25 have to do with the manner of conceiving the Holy Spirit, and chapters 40 to 49 have to do with the systematics of the Incarnation.[21]

So, what should we expect from a medieval *summa*? Lonergan answered this:

> A *summa* aimed at answering coherently some totality of *quaestiones*. The existence of each *quaestio* had to be established by quoting authorities or reasons both for a negative (*videtur quod non*) and for an affirmative (*sed contra est*) reply. The immediate task in each quaestio was the elimination of apparent contradictions whether between authorities or, on the other hand, between authoritative doctrine and the medieval mind. But besides this immediate task there was the far larger and profounder problem of making all the replies in a *summa* coherent with one another.[22]

Instructive is Aquinas's distinction between wisdom as acquired by study and wisdom as an infused gift. For example, thanks to study (*per studium*), someone can understand some elements of ethics and religion, whereas, thanks to the gift of wisdom, someone possesses an inclination towards moral and religious attitudes and thus more appreciates their significance.[23] Regarding the latter, Aquinas wrote, "It was fitting that Christ, as the most excellent of teachers, should adopt that approach (*modus*) whereby he would imprint his teaching (*doctrinam*) on the hearts of his hearers."[24]

21. Lonergan, *Method in Theology*, 311–12.
22. Lonergan, *Method in Theology*, Appendix 1: "The New Context," 371.
23. Aquinas, *Summa Theologiae*, I, q. 1, a. 6, ad 3.
24. Aquinas, *Summa Theologiae*, III, q. 42, a. 4. Translations from the

However, both movements, whether natural or supernatural, by which wisdom is imparted, are always directly caused by the Creator: "God so moves the created intellect inasmuch as he gives it the intellectual power, whether natural or superadded, impresses on the created intellect the intelligible species [namely the representation], and maintains and preserves both power and species."[25] Thomas made his view more precise when he stated: "The intellectual operation is performed by the [human] intellect in which it exists, as by a secondary cause; but it proceeds from God as from its first cause, for by him the power to understand is given to the one who understands."[26] "The intellectual light together with the likeness of the thing understood is a sufficient principle of understanding; but it is a secondary principle and depends upon the first principle."[27]

Furthermore the two kinds of wisdom are complementary. Thus Victor White, talking about the learner's limitations, noted: "The defects of his understanding, especially when confronted with the mysteries of revelation, are such that he not uncommonly needs such rational processes and convictions [of the first type of wisdom] with which, it is supposed, he is already familiar, if he is to be led to what transcends them."[28]

White also indicated that another purpose of the *Summa Theologiae* is to help the Christian educators to engage in dialogues.

> Being called to deal with all men, the *doctor veritatis catholicae* will have to deal . . . firstly, with those who already accept part but not all of the items of the *doctrina*, and secondly those who, being altogether without faith, accept none at all. Each must be met on his own ground if he is led or taught further. The position of the learner,

---

Summa are mine, although often close to those by previous translators.
25. Aquinas, *Summa Theologiae*, I, q. 105, a. 3.
26. Aquinas, *Summa Theologiae*, I, q. 105, ad 1.
27. Aquinas, *Summa Theologiae*, I, q. 105, ad 2.
28. White, *Holy Teaching*, 17.

Albert the Great and Thomas Aquinas

the beginner, is decisive for where the beginning is to be made, where contact must first be established.[29]

According to White, this is the reason why arguments must be clearly and respectfully enunciated.[30]

An Instance of Medieval Scholasticism

Having underscored the various prerequisites, which all genuine Christians possess, let us now expound Aquinas's construal of theology proper. It must be emphasized that he was a *thirteenth-century* scholastic and not an example of the subsequent, late-medieval, conceptualist and overly logical scholasticism, which began in the fourteenth century.[31] What stands out is the omnipresence of the *quaestio*, given that, in the *Summa Theologiae*, each topic is introduced by a question. So let us now examine the first question of that *Summa*.

For Aquinas, what he called "the philosophical disciplines" (namely "philosophy") are subordinated to "sacred teaching" (*sacra doctrina*), which he argues is a "science" (*scientia*).[32] It is important to understand that *doctrina* should be translated by "teaching" and not by "doctrine," as in the case of Augustine's *De Doctrina Christiana*. Thus Aquinas wrote:

> Since there is a twofold way of acquiring knowledge—by discovery and by being taught—the way of discovery is the higher, and the way of being taught is secondary. Hence it is said (Aristotle, *Ethics*, I, 4), "he indeed is the best who knows everything by himself; yet he is good who obeys the one who speaks aright."[33]

---

29. White, *Holy Teaching*, 18.

30. White refers to *Summa Theologiae*, I, q. 1, a. 8, titled "Whether Sacred Teaching is a Matter of Argument?"

31. In the present book, section titled "The Scholastic Mind," of chapter 1, I expounded those various kinds of scholasticism.

32. Aquinas, *Summa Theologiae*, q. 1, a. 1 and 2.

33. See *Summa Theologiae*, III, q. 9, a. 4, ad 1.

By being active in struggling with great and demanding thinkers, students can retain more than if they are content with merely listening to lectures.

Let us note that in the thirteenth century *sacra doctrina* meant *Christian* theology, while *theologia* meant *philosophical* theology. (Thus both Plato and Aristotle used the word *theologia* when talking about the kind of knowledge that humans can have of the Good.) Philosophy and other disciplines such as grammar, logic, etc., are ancillary to theology, while the latter is needed for two reasons. First, there must be a divine revelation that allows human beings to know their ultimate, supernatural, end, which surpasses the grasp of reason; second, even in the case of truths about God that human reason can discover, in the absence of revelation they would be known only by a few, after a long time, and mixed with many errors.[34]

In another article, Thomas maintained that sacred teaching is a matter of argument. It proceeds from its own principles, which are the articles of faith, contained in the Creed, in order to prove something else. He gives as an example the fact that St. Paul in 1 Corinthians 15, argues from the resurrection of Christ in proof of the general resurrection of the just.[35]

Furthermore, Thomas contended that Holy Scripture should use metaphors because it is natural for us to attain intellectual truths through concrete images. Citing Dionysios the Pseudo-Areopagite, he recognized that the truths are hidden behind figures, but that this fact is useful for thoughtful minds, who are thereby spurred to inquire about the meaning of the figures.[36]

He ended this question 1 of the *Summa Theologiae* with listing the four basic senses that we find in Holy Scripture: (1) historical or literal; (2) allegorical; (3) tropological or moral, and (4) anagogical.[37] He called the last three the "spiritual sense" and he

---

34. Aquinas, *Summa Theologiae*, q. 1, a. 2, and *Summa contra Gentiles*, book 1, chaps. 4 and 5, where these two points are more developed.
35. Aquinas, *Summa Theologiae*, q. 1, a. 8.
36. Aquinas, *Summa Theologiae*, q. 1, a. 9.
37. Aquinas, *Summa Theologiae*, q. 1, a. 10.

Albert the Great and Thomas Aquinas

declared that it "is based on the literal and presupposes it." First, then, following Augustine he stated that biblical commentators must first ascertain what is conveyed by assertions that are plainly stated, that is, historical or literal. Second, the allegorical sense, which is metaphorical, was explained in our chapter on Augustine. Third, the moral sense often consists in a derivation from Christ's experience to the experience of his followers, since he is the Head and they are his Body. Fourth, the anagogical sense—not to be confused with the analogical operations[38]—is the eschatological sense, with its two dimensions: the "already" present, namely the mystical, and the "not yet," which is present only in hope, namely the final vision of God.[39]

Yves Congar shed additional light on a few of Aquinas's methodological principles.[40] He summed up the latter's exegetical procedure as follows: "One should explicate a statement by its historical context, by the intention of the author, according to the problem he has posed, and the angle from which he approaches the problem, accounting for the resources the author has at his disposal."[41] Congar added, "We are better equipped to respond to difficulties that some texts can provoke when we know what question was being posed and how one arrived at this question."[42]

What should we do when we are convinced that a particular position amounts to an error? Saint Thomas helps us here, Congar wrote, by "recognizing that an erroneous formulation can coexist with a truly orthodox ideal."[43] Moreover "a discrepancy between two statements can be explained and justified by the appearance of

---

38. See Roy, *God: Polarities in Language*, forthcoming, chap. 4, section titled "Analogical Language."

39. On Aquinas's views of faith and theology, see Roy, *The Three Dimensions of Faith*, 71–90.

40. See Congar, "The Ecumenical Value and Scope of Some Hermeneutical Principles of Saint Thomas Aquinas."

41. Congar, "The Ecumenical Value," 187–88.

42. Congar, "The Ecumenical Value," 190.

43. Congar, "The Ecumenical Value," 191.

an error that forces a clarification."⁴⁴ Furthermore "when we encounter expressions that are questionable and improper, we ought to distinguish in what sense they are to be rejected and in what sense they can be better understood."⁴⁵

For instance, insofar as "the apparent discordances between the Greeks and Latins" are concerned, they "explain themselves by a difference of approach that is manifested in a difference of problematic, of conceptualization, and thus of expression."⁴⁶ In such cases, Congar thought that Thomas had applied "the principle of equivalences," namely the recognition that two positions may very well express the same faith in dissimilar cognitional frameworks.⁴⁷

I once penned:

> Aquinas introduced the notion of First Truth as the cognitive axis of faith; it is the *formal* object of faith, whereas the truths that are believed consist of its *material* object—material in the sense of subject matter. Talking about "the things to which faith assents," he tells us that "they include not only God, but also many other things, which, nevertheless, do not come under the assent of faith except as bearing some relation to God."⁴⁸

Congar explained, "Things concerning Christ's human nature, the sacraments of the church, or any creatures whatever, come under faith insofar as by them we are directed to God and inasmuch as we assent to them on account of the divine Truth."⁴⁹ So there is an "order" or an "ordering" (*ordo*) according to Aquinas,⁵⁰ namely a "hierarchy" among the principal objects of belief: God as Trinity, the Creation, the Incarnation, the Passion and

---

44. Congar, "The Ecumenical Value," 193.
45. Congar, "The Ecumenical Value," 193.
46. "The Ecumenical Value," 194.
47. "The Ecumenical Value," 196; see 200.
48. Roy, *Revelation in a Pluralistic World*, 206–7, quoting Aquinas, *Summa Theologiae*, II–II, q. 1, a. 1, ad 1.
49. Congar's Preface to William Henn, *The Hierarchy of Truths according to Yves Congar, O.P.*, xi; see also x.
50. Aquinas, *Summa Theologiae*, II–II, q. 1, a. 7.

Resurrection, the Redemption, the Church, and the sacraments—all truths of the faith being mentioned by Vatican II.

Concluding Remarks

Perhaps we should go to Augustine and Albert as awakeners, that is, as thinkers who stir up their students' interest by raising questions and adumbrating perspectives, and we should go to Aquinas for his analytical and synthetic gifts.[51] Interestingly, after the death of Aquinas, Albert defended his pupil's positions; the *doctor universalis* and the *doctor angelicus* were in unison.[52]

However, more importantly than those two characterizations, both Albert's and Thomas's methods conjoin intellectuality and affectivity, as well as desire to understand and prayerfulness.

I hope that the examples of Augustine, Albert, and Thomas have made us realize that pre-modern thinkers practised an exegesis that was indeed critical, albeit in their own ways.[53] Nonetheless we must admit that, since the eighteenth century, modern thinkers have brought into the discussion a greater sense of historicity concerning text-interpretation. I shall expound some of their contributions in the next chapters.

---

51. The same thing can be said about Chenu, the awakener, who deeply influenced Congar, his student, whose main gift was the capacity to collect, examine, and draw conclusions from historical facts with more precision than Chenu.

52. Regarding this fact, see Tugwell, *Albert & Thomas*, 26–27.

53. See Dulles, *The Craft of Theology*, 3–15, on what he termed the "precritial, critical, paracritical, countercritical, and postcritical" fashions of reading the Bible and the Christian traditions.

5

Friedrich Schleiermacher

This chapter and the next will introduce the thought of a two Protestants, one in the nineteenth century and one in the twentieth, whose writings on text-interpretation rank among the most important: Friedrich Schleiermacher and Paul Ricœur.

Schleiermacher (1768–1834) has been correctly dubbed "the Father of Liberal Protestantism." He has the merit of having synthesized the views of the Enlightenment and Romanticism, to some extent successfully.[1] Throughout his career he explicated a conception of hermeneutics in which the thought's structure of his Enlightenment predecessors, especially Kant, turned out to be profoundly modified.

In his *Brief Outline of Theology as a Field of Study*, Schleiermacher begins by defining theology as follows:

> Theology is a positive science, the parts of which join into a cohesive whole only through their common relation to a particular mode of faith, that is, a particular way of being conscious of God. Thus, the various parts

---

1. See Roy, "Schleiermacher's Epistemology," 25–46, and *Transcendent Experiences*, 47–68.

Friedrich Schleiermacher

of Christian theology belong together only by virtue of their relation to Christianity.[2]

The translator comments: "The entire outline is about this definition. Three features of the definition ["positive," "science," and "Christianity"] stand out, though, and these are best explained in terms of §§1–19 of *Christian Faith*, his systematic presentation of doctrine for the evangelical Church of his time."[3]

Consequently Schleiermacher differentiates his *Brief Outline* into three parts: "historical theology" (positive accounts of the Bible and the subsequent traditions), "philosophical theology" (the fundamental principles of scientific theology, which come from philosophy), and "practical theology" (the concrete enhancement of the Church as a service).

Taking into consideration this broad status of a theology that Schleiermacher situates with respect to history, philosophy, and other disciplines—all of which are integrated into theology –, we shall examine hermeneutical questions regarding his interpretative method as applied to texts, in particular to historical, philosophical, and practical texts.

Questions and Method

In his Introduction to Schleiermacher's *Hermeneutics*, James Duke wrote: "How is a text to be understood? How does understanding itself occur? These questions lie at the heart of Schleiermacher's theory of interpretation, his hermeneutics. Fundamental to his view is the conviction that the first question can be answered only in terms of the second."[4] Both questions have to do with "understanding" (*Verstehen*); logically, however, the prior one is the issue of interpersonal understanding, and the next one is the issue

---

2. Schleiermacher, *Brief Outline of Theology as a Field of Study*, §1; I refer to the paragraphs as indicated by Schleiermacher and by Tice.

3. Schleiermacher, *Brief Outline*, Editor's General introduction, ix.

4. Translators' Introduction, in Schleiermacher, *Hermeneutics: The Handwritten Manuscripts*, 1.

of text-understanding. Thanks to tackling these two questions, Schleiermacher developed a method for correct understanding.

His interpretative method is comprised of two fundamental phases: first, a "universal element" (also named "the general,"), and second, a "particular element" (also variously named "the specific," "the grammatical," "the technical" or "the psychological interpretation," according to his successive manuscripts).[5] Schleiermacher cautioned about the error of imagining that our two principal hermeneutical activities would be successive: "The two operations are combined in the actual application."[6] However, within the phase, which is subdivided into two steps, the grammatical interpretation remains impersonal, whereas the technical interpretation concerns the individuality of the author that one is interpreting.[7]

The universal element consists of several requirements: a preliminary knowledge of human beings, a preliminary knowledge of the subject matter, the general linguistic rules that are applied, and the initial sense of the whole of a text, all of which guide the construal of any part of the text: "Even if the interpreter does not recognize the individuality of a work in its overall organization, the organization of the whole is still the basis for the technical interpretation of the various parts because even at this point the general laws of combination are operative."[8]

---

5. Schleiermacher, *Hermeneutics*, 45 and *passim* throughout the several manuscripts included in that compilation by Kimmerle. In Schleiermacher, *Hermeneutics and Criticism and Other Writings* [a slightly different title and a different compilation], at xxxix, Bowie points out that the word "Kunst"... "oscillates in meaning between 'technique,' or 'method,' and 'art.'" Note that this more recent translation is different from the Duke and Forstman's translation, although the German texts that have been translated are substantially the same.

6. Schleiermacher, *Hermeneutics: The Handwritten Manuscripts*, 69; for a point-by-point comparison between the two principal operations, see 161–73.

7. According to Bowie in his Introduction to *Hermeneutics and Criticism and Other Writings*, xxx.

8. Schleiermacher, *Hermeneutics: The Handwritten Manuscripts*, 58.

Friedrich Schleiermacher

Interpretation: Grammatical and Technical

There is a clear similarity between the grammatical and the technical interpretation: as in the grammatical inquiry, the technical inquiry takes limits into consideration; in the first operation one takes the general linguistic limits into consideration, while in the second operation one focuses on the limits of the writer as a unique individual. Exactly knowing how authors use their language rules out many misunderstandings by indicating the limits of what authors can convey in terms of meaning.

Still, there is also a difference. The grammatical interpretation is defined as follows: "It is the art of finding the precise sense (*Sinn*) of a given statement from its language and with the help of its language. . . . One should construe the meaning from the total pre-given value of language and the heritage common to the author and his reader."[9]

The technical interpretation has to do with discovering the general consistency of a piece of writing.

> Technical interpretation is chiefly concerned with the over-all coherence and with its relation to the universal laws for combining thoughts. . . . In technical interpretation the unity of the work, its theme, is viewed as the dynamic principle impelling the author, and the basic features of the composition are viewed as his distinctive nature, revealing itself.[10]

Schleiermacher explicates:

> Technical interpretation involves two methods: a divinatory and a comparative. . . . By leading the interpreter to transform himself, so to speak, into the author, the divinatory method seeks to gain an immediate comprehension of the author as an individual. The comparative method proceeds by subsuming the author under a general type.

---

9. Schleiermacher, *Hermeneutics: The Handwritten Manuscripts*, 70; see also 117–47.

10. Schleiermacher, *Hermeneutics: The Handwritten Manuscripts*, 69 and 147; see also 147–51.

Methodologies in Systematic Theology

It then tries to find his distinctive traits by comparing him with the others of the same general type.[11]

Talking about "divination," Jean Grondin explains:

> By this term he refers not to a sacred gift but merely the process of guessing (*divinare*). At the point when the fundamentally comparative means of grammatical interpretation leave us at a loss—that is, when it is not the commonness but the uniqueness of a particular style that is to be elucidated—then often enough we simply have to guess what the author was trying to say.[12]

The Issue of Psychologizing

Heinz Kimmerle, the German editor of Schleiermacher's *Hermeneutik*, was critical of Wilhelm Dilthey, who forcefully and excessively accentuated the "psychological" character of Schleiermacher's doctrine of interpretation.[13] It is true that in his later reflections on interpretation, Schleiermacher began using the

---

11. Schleiermacher, *Hermeneutics: The Handwritten Manuscripts*, 150. In *Truth and Method*, Gadamer states that there is "the spirit of rationalism" (195) in Schleiermacher, expressed by "putting oneself on the same level as the author" (191); see the section titled "Schleiermacher's Project of a Universal Hermeneutics," 184–97. Gadamer thereby suggests that, in Schleiermacher's conception, the *interpreter* exercises a certain mastery over the *author*, since the former little by little becomes more conscious than the latter of the actual meaning of the text. I have serious doubts about this aspect of Gadamer's reading of Schleiermacher; after all, Schleiermacher asserted, at *Hermeneutics*, 149, "what we do understand is always subject to correction."

12. Grondin, *Introduction to Philosophical Hermeneutics*, 71. Such a probable hypothesis is what is sometimes dubbed "an educated guess." For his nuanced presentation and assessment of Schleiermacher's thought, see 67–75. Let us note that Grondin, who studied in Germany under Gadamer and is greatly indebted to his mentor and friend, nonetheless does not quite accept the latter's criticisms of Schleiermacher (see 72–75).

13. About the problem of correctly interpreting Schleiermacher on hermeneutics while distancing oneself from Dilthey's view of it, see Heinz Kimmerle, "Foreword to the German Edition" and "Afterword of 1968," in *Hermeneutics: The Handwritten Manuscripts*, 19–20 and 229–34.

adjective "psychological" as a synonym for "technical." He declared: "Psychological interpretation is easier and more certain when the interpreter and the author combine thoughts in the same way and when the interpreter has a detailed knowledge of the author's thoughts."[14] In other words, his method aims at reaching a kind of identification with the mind of an author.

Both Hans-Georg Gadamer, Kimmerle's mentor, and Kimmerle himself mistakenly adopted a construing of Schleiermacher through Dilthey's eyes.[15] Indeed, contrary to what they believed, "divining" is not, for Schleiermacher, the result of intuitions. Bowie explains that it is "the ability to arrive at interpretations without definitive rules," hence an "art, because it cannot be fully carried out in terms of rules," a "free activity, which allows us to transcend such rules in order both to understand in a new context where it is not self-evident from the context that the rule is applicable, and to articulate the world in new and individual ways."[16]

Indeed Schleiermacher speaks of a series of "operations," (he repeatedly mentioned "operations"), that is, in my own rephrasing, the personal, intimate, not necessarily shared murmuring of searchers juggling with successive hypotheses and saying to themselves words such as "perhaps the author means A" or "perhaps the author means B," and so forth. Such operations are activities, and they in no way amount to non-discursive intuitions.

Coda: Phenomenology and Hermeneutics

As a transition from this chapter on Schleiermacher to the next chapter on Lonergan, let us characterize phenomenology and hermeneutics.

---

14. Schleiermacher, *Hermeneutics: The Handwritten Manuscripts*, 223.

15. For a negative comment on "the standard misconception of Schleiermacher's hermeneutics" (i.e. by Gadamer), see Bowie's "Note on the text and the translation" in *Hermeneutics and Criticism and Other Writings*, xxxvii.

16. Bowie, Introduction to *Hermeneutics and Criticism and Other Writings*, x and xi.

Phenomenology was hermeneutics' predecessor. Since the great philosopher Edmund Husserl (1859–1938), phenomenology has been understood by his disciples as beginning with observable data that are called "phenomena." In Greek, the noun *phainomenon* is "what has been lit up," from the verb *phainein*, "to shine." The phenomena are modes of human behavior that shine, namely that appear and that can be examined and critically assessed.

Let us preface our characterization of hermeneutics with a quotation from Gadamer, whose conception echoes the one that Schleiermacher proposed:

> There is no hermeneutic method. All the methods developed by scholarship can be hermeneutically profitable. . . . Hermeneutics means not so much a procedure as the attitude of a person who wants to understand someone else, or who wants to understand a linguistic expression as a reader or listener. But this always means understanding *this* person, *this* text.[17]

The noun "hermeneutics" comes from the Greek god Hermes, seen as the inventor of language and the messenger of the gods; hence it is the science that studies interpretation of discourses, which are either oral or written. There is also the Greek verb *hermeneuein*, "to interpret." Its principal *modern* practitioners are Friedrich Schleiermacher, Martin Heidegger (1889–1976), Hans-Georg Gadamer (1900–2002), Paul Ricœur (1913–2005), and Jürgen Habermas (born in 1929).

The difference between phenomenology and hermeneutics is that the former (as in Husserl, but not in all of his disciples) consists in highlighting the fundamental structures of human consciousness and thinking, whereas the latter consists in correctly reading classical texts and/or correctly making sense of human actions and interactions, namely of human experience.

The hermeneutical circle operates within hermeneutics. Therefore I will report how several thinkers defined the hermeneutical circle.

---

17. Hans-Georg Gadamer, *"Who Am I and Who Are You?" and other essays*, 161.

Friedrich Schleiermacher

In *The Symbolism of Evil*, Paul Ricœur underlines the inevitability of that circle: "The circle can be stated bluntly: 'We must understand in order to believe, but we must believe in order to understand.' The circle is not a vicious circle, still less a moral one; it is a living and stimulating circle."[18] A bit further on, he explains: "These reflections on the 'circle' in hermeneutics put us on the road to a *philosophical* hermeneutics, but they do not take its place. The awareness of that 'circle' is only a necessary stage by which we pass from a simple 're-enactment' without belief to autonomous 'thought.'"[19]

Bernard Lonergan characterizes it in these words:

> The meaning of a text is an intentional entity. It is a unity that is unfolded through parts, sections, chapters, paragraphs, sentences, words. We can grasp the unity, the whole, only through the parts. At the same time the parts are determined in their meaning by the whole which each part partially reveals. Such is the hermeneutic circle.[20]

On his part Charles Taylor describes it as follows:

> This is one way of trying to express what has been called the "hermeneutical circle." What we are trying to establish is a certain reading of texts or expressions, and what we appeal to as our grounds for this reading can only be other readings. The circle can also be put in terms of part-whole relations: we are trying to establish a reading for the whole text, and for this we appeal to readings of its partial expressions; and yet because we are dealing with meaning, with making sense, where expressions only make sense or not in relation to others, the readings of partial expressions depend on those of others, and ultimately of the whole.[21]

---

18. Ricœur, *The Symbolism of Evil*, 351. *La Symbolique du mal* is volume 3 of his *Philosophie de la volonté*
19. Ricœur, *The Symbolism of Evil*, 353.
20. Lonergan, *Method in Theology*, 151.
21. Taylor, *Philosophical Papers*, vol. 2, 18.

In theology, this circular movement has been frequently construed as the following correlation: human experience as preceding faith, and faith as responding to the concerns of human experience. In that interaction, experience shapes the perspective and the expression of any concrete faith, while faith questions, rectifies, enriches, and expands experience. An instance of this twofold movement is the reciprocal influence between philosophy of God and revelation of God. Consequently, there is neither 'pure' experience nor 'pure' faith; both are interpreted and reinterpreted by human intellects. Moreover, both are to be seen within the context of human lives, which are molded by a cognitive-affective framework.

Concluding Remarks

Let us conclude this chapter on Schleiermacher by quoting him again: "Understanding is an unending task. . . .That thought is to be treated neither as something objective nor as a thing, but as an act (*Factum*)."[22] He observes also, "When rightly understood, the infinite significance of the Holy Scriptures is not in contradiction to its hermeneutical limitations."[23] We shall see, with Lonergan and Ricœur, that the interpretation of a text, especially of a religious one, ever remains unfinished.

---

22. Schleiermacher, *Hermeneutics: The Handwritten Manuscripts*, 41 and 43.

23. Schleiermacher, *Hermeneutics: The Handwritten Manuscripts*, 55.

6

Bernard Lonergan

In my opinion, Bernard Lonergan (1904–1984) was the best Catholic philosopher-theologian of the twentieth century. The strength of his methodology rested on his cognitional theory, his functional specialties as constitutive of theological method, his two exposés on interpretation (the second one bringing in a notion of dialectic), his adoption of historicity and his consequent rejection of extrinsicism, and finally his understanding of interpersonal dialogue—all of which exercise a vital function in theology. To complete my elucidation of those many components of his methodology, I will insert a comparison between his views and Schleiermacher's views on hermeneutics.[1]

Human Intentionality

To understand Lonergan's cognitional theory, one has to go to his first book, *Insight*, which develops a "moving viewpoint" towards an appropriation of one's cognitional operations[2]; such an

---

1. One can find a good guide in *Lonergan's Hermeneutics*, Subject Index, at "Hermeneutical," "Hermeneutics," "Interpretation", "Interpretational," and "Interpreter."

2. Lonergan, *Insight*, Index, at "Viewpoint of *Insight*," 873.

appropriation is described more fully in his second masterwork, titled *Method in Theology*.³ Explicitly acknowledging one's intellectual and affective activities is a prerequisite if students are to achieve the kind of personal integration mentioned in my Introduction.

Cognitional theory requires a self-consciousness that takes up metaphorical and allegorical practices and goes beyond them. It consists in an intellectual self-appropriation that issues forth into an objective account of one's subjectivity, namely an epistemology. The latter is comprised of what Lonergan calls four "levels" of human intentionality. Here is the way I would describe them.

The word *Intentionalität*, which comes from the Austrian philosopher Franz Brentano and was adopted by the German philosopher Edmund Husserl, refers to a tension towards reality—a tension that constitutes the human being's very life. Drawing on Thomas Aquinas' epistemology, Lonergan describes how intentionality, as a dynamism, unfolds on four levels. A principal activity characterizes each level: experience, understanding, judgment, and decision. Each of these levels activates many other operations which I don't have the space to analyse here.

Those levels may be sketched in this schema, subdivided into two indispensable movements:

4. Decision: 4.2 Vertical → Infinite Love
   4.1 Horizontal → Finite values

3. Judgment → Truths

2. Understanding → Meanings

1. Experience: 1.2 Sensory Representations
   1.1 Sense Data

The human subject moves through these four levels in two directions: in an upwards movement and in a downwards movement.

---

3. The results of self-appropriation are expounded in *Method in Theology*, CWBL, vol. 14, especially 7–54.

1.1 In the first case, from lower to higher, one starts by taking in data from the senses (sight, hearing, etc.), which in today's scientific world are enhanced electronically. While we share this first level with animals, the other levels are specifically human since they are rooted in acts of questioning. One is able to move from one level to the next through questions.

1.2 Thus one moves from level one to level two by asking questions related to the data such as: What is that? What does that mean? How does that work? Why does that happen this way? The answers to these questions are insights, which are acts of understanding, and are expressed in interrelated concepts that form hypotheses.

1.3 The hypotheses of this second level spontaneously lead us to ask questions of another kind, which allow a critical detachment with respect to our hypotheses. One then progresses to the third level when one asks: Is that really the case? Is that true? Which hypothesis best reflects reality? The answers given are for the most part only probable: they are judgments about reality, which is known in a manner that is imperfect, open to revision, and nonetheless probably correct.

1.4 Finally, questions of yet a different kind lead us to progress to the fourth level, that is, to the topmost level: What needs to be done in that situation? Is there a good that can emerge? Which action is worthy of being undertaken? And, once a relevant value has been identified, must I be consistent and commit myself to it as well as to the people for whom this value has meaning?

The movement I have just described is from lower to higher. In addition, human intentionality also acts from higher to lower.

2.4 This second movement starts at the fourth level, the level of values, of love, of commitment to others. Here one lives within a horizon, that is a set of interests, a particular sensitivity to aspects of one's life.

2.3 This basic state enables us to more easily accept, at the third level, truths that agree with that which we value, at the fourth level.

2.2 Next, as we progressively accept these truths, we gain a deeper understanding of their importance, at the second level.

2.1 Finally, at the first level, we express that which we hold dear (fourth level), consider true (third level) and find meaningful (second level). We then become both creators and communicators of data, which we hope are intelligible, true and value-laden, through the use of the many forms of language at our disposal: day-to-day or technical, commonplace or artistic, etc.

Lonergan's method embraces these four broad types of operations that recur in various ways in a huge variety of situations. It includes not only the data of sense, but also the data of human consciousness, which makes self-appropriation possible.[4] Far from being restricted to particular domains, it applies to all fields of knowledge, with the transpositions required by each special method.

Lonergan admits a more elementary characterization of human thinking because ordinary people express themselves metaphorically. There is nonetheless a process that naturally unfolds as "metaphor is revised and contracted myth and that myth is anticipated and expanded metaphor." Then one passes from "existing viewpoints" to "new viewpoints."

> There is then an allegorical aspect of myth. It is an aspect that emerges when myth is conceived as a solution to a problem of expression. . . . We have described myth as an untutored effort of the desire to know, to grasp and formulate the nature of things. In the measure that such an effort tries to free itself from its fetters, myth attains an allegorical significance.[5]

Readers need allegory if they are to identify themselves with heroes that can be imitated or repudiated. Besides, let us observe that for Lonergan "myth," which portrays various protagonists, is both helpful at the beginning of human thinking and yet insufficient in the long run.[6] Consequently the philosophic-theological enterprise needs much more, namely cognitional theory.

---

4. See Lonergan, *Insight*, 95–96 and 268.

5. Lonergan, *Insight*, 569.

6. See Roy, *God: Polarities in Language*, forthcoming, chap. 11, section titled "A Dialectical Treatment of the Issue."

Bernard Lonergan

Functional Specialties

Lonergan's eight functional specialties exactly follow the two movements of the four levels of intentionality:

		MEDIATING THEOLOGY/*ORATIONE OBLIQUA*	MEDIATED THEOLOGY/*ORATIONE RECTA*		
		Revealing the religious situation/Knowledge of the Body of Christ	Knowledge of God as He is known through the whole Christ		
4. DECISION	APOLOGETICS →	⁴DIALECTIC	⁵FOUNDATIONS	← FUNDAMENTAL
3. JUDGEMENT	CHURCH HISTORY/ HIST. OF SALVATION →	³HISTORY	⁶DOCTRINES	← DOGMATIC
2. UNDERSTANDING	COMMENTARIES/ MONOGRAPHS →	²INTERPRETATION	⁷SYSTEMATICS	← SPECULATIVE
1. EXPERIENCING	TEXTUAL CRITICISM →	¹RESEARCH	⁸COMMUNICATIONS	← PASTORAL

↑ DIMENSION OF LEVELS
DIMENSION OF SEQUENCE/CHRONOLOGY ⟶

Prepared by Janusz Dubiel, B.A.(Hon.), B.Th., M.A., M.A.Th.(in progress), November 2007, TH4900, Dominican University College. To be revised if nec.

Given what has been said before, here and in former chapters, the meaning of those theological functions should be pretty much evident. However we need to pay attention to two of them, which are the linchpin of the whole theological enterprise, namely "Dialectic" and "Foundations." The reason is that these two functions elucidate the essential role of the scholar and of the student, that is, the subjective conditions of those who are doing theology. The subjective conditions are the religious, moral, and intellectual conversions, which will be delineated presently.[7]

A First Exposé on Interpretation

Lonergan has two systematic exposés on interpretation. His first exposé can be found in a section of *Insight* titled "The Truth of Interpretation."[8] There he insists on the difficulties of correctly

---

7. On the conversions, "Dialectic," and "Foundations," see Roy, "The Viability of the Category of Religious Experience in Bernard Lonergan's Theology," 99–117.

8. Lonergan, *Insight*, 585–617.

establishing the intellectual situation of the audiences that an interpreter wishes to address. Because the audiences are various, this process is bound to be difficult and consequently requires attentiveness and flexibility on the part of the interpreter. Lonergan explains:

> It may very well happen that any simple interpretation is correct, that it hits off for a contemporary audience the principal insight communicated by the original document.... For analogous to common sense there is a historical sense. Just as we by common sense can know how our contemporaries would or would not speak or act in any of a series or ordinary and typical situations, so the scholar by a long familiarity with the documents and monuments of another age and by an ever increasing accumulation of complementary insights can arrive at a participation of the common sense of another period, and by this historical sense can tell how the men and women of that time would or would not speak or act in certain types of situation.[9]

Nonetheless the interpreter must recognize that his task is aggravated by the presence of individual and collective forms of bias:

> However, just as our common sense is open to individual, group, and general bias, so also is the historical sense [of the interpreter]. Moreover, just as our common sense cannot analyze itself or criticize itself or arrive at an abstract formulation of its central nucleus, so also the historical sense is limited in a similar fashion; both are more likely to be correct in pronouncing verdicts than in assigning exact and convincing reasons for them. But if interpretation is to be scientific, then the grounds for the interpretation have to be assignable.[10]

We therefore need a robustly critical kind of interpretation, which Lonergan will rename "dialectic" in his *Method in Theology*.

---

9. Lonergan, *Insight*, 987.

10. Lonergan did not find necessary in this context to mention the dramatic bias, which he explained earlier in *Insight*; on forms of bias, see *Insight*, 214–23 and 244–61. See also Roy, *Engaging the Thought of Bernard Lonergan*, 218–23.

Bernard Lonergan

A Second Exposé on Interpretation

Lonergan's *second* exposé on interpretation is found in chapter 7 of *Method in Theology*, titled "Interpretation."[11] At the outset he defines hermeneutics as distinct from exegesis:

> I shall follow a common enough terminology and understand by 'hermeneutics' principles of interpretation and by 'exegesis' the application of the principles to a given task. The task to be envisaged will be the interpretation of a text, but the presentation will be so general that it can be applied to any exegetical task.[12]

As indicated in our chapter 5, like Schleiermacher Lonergan speaks of "operations." For him, those operations consist of (1) understanding the object to which the text refers, (2) understanding the words employed, (3) understanding the author, and (4) understanding oneself.[13] Note that these four operations do not correspond to the four levels of intentionality.

Lonergan has this to say about checking out and ascertaining the correctness of one's interpretation of a text:

> To judge the correctness of one's understanding of a text raises the problem of context, of the hermeneutical circle, of the relativity of the totality of relevant data, of the possible relevance of more remote inquiries, of the limitations to be placed on the scope of one's interpretation.
>
> To state what one judges to be the correct understanding of the text raises the question of the precise task

---

11. In *Lonergan, Hermeneutics, & Theological Method*, Donna Teevan correctly argued that Lonergan's thought possesses a hermeneutical aspect, and she helpfully presents what I am calling here my "first exposé on interpretation," but she has very little to say about what I am calling my "second exposé on interpretation," namely dialectic; see Teevan's book, 115–17; I was surprised that the word "dialectic" is not in her Index.

12. Lonergan, *Method in Theology*, 146. This twofold enterprise goes back to Schleiermacher, as we saw in our preceding chapter.

13. Lonergan, *Method in Theology*, 147–54.

of the exegete, of the categories he is to employ, of the language he is to speak.[14]

One has not only to know the language employed and something about the objects treated in a text, but one has also to find out what are the objects that the author has in mind. "The exegete also learns from texts something that otherwise he would not know. . . . Such knowledge, of course, is general and potential. . . . The greater the exegete's resources, the greater the likelihood that he will be able to enumerate all possible interpretations assign to each its proper measure of probability."[15]

In contrast to the controversialist, who "sets about his triumphant demonstration of the author's errors and absurdities," "the interpreter considers the possibility that he himself is at fault. He reads further. He rereads."[16] At some point he discovers the real meaning of the author's words and sentences. This long process takes time and patience.

"The problem, now, is a matter not of understanding the object or the words but of understanding the author himself, his nation, language, time, culture, way of life, and cast of mind." The interpreter must now "acquire an understanding of other people's common sense." Lonergan adds:

> But, just as common sense itself is a matter of understanding what to say and what to do in any of a series of situations that commonly arise, so understanding another's common sense is a matter of understanding what he would say and what he would do in any of the situations that commonly arose in his place and time.[17]

---

14. Lonergan, *Method in Theology*, 148. For details, see Meyer, *Critical Realism and the New Testament* and *Reality and Illusion in New Testament Scholarship*.

15. Lonergan, *Method in Theology*, 148–49. Paying attention to these operations requires rejecting the erroneous "principle of the empty head," namely a kind of "naïve intuitionism" that Lonergan ironically summarized as follows: "In brief, the less one knows, the better an exegete one will be" (149).

16. Lonergan, *Method in Theology*, 150.

17. Lonergan, *Method in Theology*, 152.

Bernard Lonergan

Lonergan explains: "The major texts, the classics, in religion, letters, philosophy, theology, not only are beyond the initial horizon of their interpreters but also may demand an intellectual, moral, religious conversion of the interpreter." And he comments: "This is the existential dimension of the problem of hermeneutics. It lies at the very root of the perennial divisions of mankind in their views on reality, morality, and religion."[18]

Lonergan's next contribution to hermeneutics is his chapter 10, titled "Dialectic."[19] It has to do with the interpreters' self-understanding. It deals with incompatible views, namely of oppositions among interpreters that are more than the plurality of views that are either complementary or genetic. Such oppositions are dialectical and must be clarified by paying attention to horizons that depend on the presence or absence—total or partial—of the threefold conversion.

Understanding oneself requires a triple conversion, intellectual, moral, and religious.[20] Intellectual conversion consists in upturning one's view of human knowledge, and consequently of reality and objectivity; one then has entered into the world mediated by meaning as one no longer envisions knowing as a looking—like children do in their world of immediacy. Moral conversion radically modifies the criterion of one's decisions as no longer based on satisfactions to value. "It consists in opting for the truly good, even for value against satisfaction when value and satisfaction conflict."[21] It takes place when people decide to be fully responsible. And finally, religious conversion "is other-worldly falling in love. It is total and permanent self-surrender without conditions, qualifications, reservations."[22]

---

18. Lonergan, *Method in Theology*, 152–53.

19. Lonergan's "dialectic" amounts to incompatibilities between positions whereas Ricœur's "dialectic" amounts to complementarities among reading methods, as will be noted in my chapter 7, and among other concepts.

20. For a description of the conversions, see Lonergan, *Method in Theology*, 223–29.

21. Lonergan, *Method in Theology*, 226.

22. Lonergan, *Method in Theology*, 226.

It is on the fourth level of interiority that dialectic operates. "But besides so intellectual a hermeneutics [on the first three levels], there also is an evaluative hermeneutics."[23] We must take account of this problem: "The presence or absence of intellectual, of moral, of religious conversion gives rise to dialectically opposed horizons. While complementary or genetic differences can be bridged, dialectical differences involve mutual repudiation."[24] The solution consists of identifying both positions and counter-positions, of developing the former and of reversing the latter. "Positions are statements compatible with intellectual, moral, and religious conversion.... Counter-positions are statements incompatible with intellectual, or moral, or religious conversion."[25]

He adds:

> Positions and counter-positions... are to be apprehended in their proper dialectical character. Human authenticity is not some pure quality, some serene freedom from all oversights, all misunderstanding, all mistakes, all sins. Rather it consists in a withdrawal from unauthenticity, and the withdrawal is never a permanent achievement.[26]

He comments:

> Indeed, the basic idea of the method we are trying to develop takes its stand on discovering what human authenticity is and showing how to appeal to it. It is not an infallible method, for men easily are unauthentic, but it is a powerful method, for man's deepest need and most prized achievement is authenticity.[27]

---

23. Lonergan, *Method in Theology*, 231.
24. Lonergan, *Method in Theology*, 232–33.
25. Lonergan, *Method in Theology*, 234.
26. Lonergan, *Method in Theology*, 237.
27. Lonergan, *Method in Theology*, 238.

Bernard Lonergan

Historicity versus Extrinsicism

According to Lonergan, the historical method is a sound departure from the assumption that among civilized Christians there ought to be one culture and one theology, and this assumption he dubbed "classicism."[28] What he called "the historical-mindedness" appeared in the eighteenth century and expanded in the nineteenth; it was progressively, albeit not fully, adopted by the Catholic Church in the twentieth century. He wrote: "To understand a doctrine is to understand the history of the doctrine."[29] He added:

> Also included under 'proper object' is the fact that understanding a doctrine and understanding the history of the doctrine are mutually dependent sets of operations that illumine each other. . . . Whoever does not understand the history of a doctrine cannot grasp exactly what needs to be developed, what is already complete, or the connection of the elements."[30]

As Maurice Blondel had done at the end of the nineteenth century, Lonergan, in 1963, warned against the presence of what Blondel dubbed "extrinsicism" in theology[31]:

> If theology has its own proper method, it is not just a mixture assembled from other sciences. But to grasp this entails withdrawing *from* extrinsicism with regard to both truth and concepts and withdrawing *to* the pre-conceptual, pre-judicial, pre-predicative realm, that is, to understanding, which is experienced just as much as are hearing and seeing. Then theology will have its own proper principle, which is not reason and not faith, but reason illumined by faith."[32]

---

28. See Roy, *Engaging the Thought of Bernard Lonergan*, Study 7, titled "Neither Classicism nor Relativism," 102–17. See also Roy, "Thomas Aquinas since Vatican II," 109–15.
29. "The Method of Theology Spring 1963," 6.
30. "The Method of Theology Spring 1963," 8.
31. See Roy, *Engaging the Thought of Bernard Lonergan*, 156–57.
32. "The Method of Theology Spring 1963," 6–7.

He explained:

> Extrinsicism is not concerned with fostering and developing intelligence, but with terms, propositions, and syllogisms. Decadence sets in when theology is about conclusions—that is, it does not understand sources or theological principles; theology becomes a rhetorical exercise; theses from tradition are proved from the scriptures, the popes, the Fathers, theologians, and reason."[33]

Human nature comprises two fundamental components: one of them is a variable, historicity, which explains the multiplicity of cultures; the other component is a constant, namely natural right, which is made up of the transcultural dynamisms of the person.[34] Unfortunately a lack of articulation between these two fundamental components impoverishes theological thinking; and a unilateral emphasis either on historical studies or on dogmas generates either a neglect of an intelligible unification of doctrines, or else a reject—tacit or voluble—of historical consciousness.[35]

Interpersonal Dialogue

In *Method in Theology*, Lonergan has a chapter on meaning, which sheds light on the relevance of interpersonal dialogue in his overal theological method. That chapter 3 begins with two sections on intersubjectivity.[36] In the first one, he states:

> Prior to the 'we' that results from the mutual love of an 'I' and a 'thou,' there is the earlier 'we' that precedes the distinction of subjects and survives its oblivion. This prior 'we' is vital and functional.... It is as if 'we' were

---

33. "The Method of Theology Spring 1963," 57. On extrinsicism, see "Beyond Extrinsicism and Immanentism," 108–22, and *Method in Theology*, Appendix 1, §7, "The New Theology," 377.

34. See Lonergan, *A Third Collection*, CWBL, 163–76.

35. See Lonergan, *Method in Theology*, 145.

36. Lonergan, *Method in Theology*, 55–59, and *Philosophical and Theological Papers 1958–1964*, 160–82.

members of one another prior to our distinctions of each from the others.[37]

To clarify intersubjectivity, Lonergan has recourse to Max Scheler's definition of "community of feeling" and of "fellow-feeling":

> In community of feeling, two or more persons respond in parallel fashion to the same object. In fellow-feeling, a first person responds to an object, and a second responds to the manifested feeling of the first. So community of feeling would be illustrated by the sorrow felt by both parents for their dead child. But fellow-feeling would be felt by a third party moved by their sorrow.[38]

Lonergan provides another illustration: "In community worship, there is community of feeling inasmuch as worshipers are similarly concerned with God, but there is fellow-feeling inasmuch as some are moved to devotion by the prayerful attitude of others."[39] He adds, "Besides the intersubjectivity of action and of feeling, there also are intersubjective communications of meaning."[40] Not always being successful, such linguistic communications need becoming acquainted with the common sense of other people. Later, still in *Method in Theology*, he develops this point:

> The self-correcting process of learning is not only the way in which we acquire our own common sense but also the way in which we acquire the understanding of other people's common sense. Even with our contemporaries with the same language, culture, and station in life, we not only understand things with them but also understand things in our own way and, at the same time, their different way of understanding the same things.... We can come to an understanding of our fellows' understanding,

---

37. Lonergan, *Method in Theology*, 56. This quotation anticipates the marvellous *The I in We*, which is the title of one of Honneth's books.
38. Lonergan, *Method in Theology*, 56.
39. Lonergan, *Method in Theology*, 56.
40. Lonergan, *Method in Theology*, 57.

a commonsense grasp of the ways in which we understand not with them but them.[41]

Non-verbal communication is also important. After proposing a brief phenomenology of smiles, Lonergan remarks:

> A smile does have a meaning. It is not just a certain combination of movements of lips, facial muscles, eyes. It is a combination with a meaning. Because that meaning is different from the meaning of a frown, a scowl, a stare, a glare, a snicker, a laugh, it is named a smile.[42]

Moreover he distinguishes the smile from the linguistic meaning:

> Linguistic meaning tends to be univocal, but smiles have a wide variety of different meanings. There are smiles of recognition, of welcome, of friendship, of love, of joy, of delight, of contentment, of satisfaction, of amusement, of refusal, of contempt. Smiles may be ironic, sardonic, enigmatic, glad or sad, fresh or weary, eager or resigned.[43]

Incidentally Lonergan was aware of Schutz's first book when he wrote:

> The intentional style [of social science] is phenomenological: its subjective dimensions are the constituting intentionalities of embodied consciousness; its objective dimensions are the forms in which the world appears for this consciousness. This style was transported from Vienna to America by Alfred Schutz who, six years before emigrating, had composed *Der sinnhafte Aufbau der socialen Welt*.[44]

---

41. Lonergan, *Method in Theology*, 152.
42. Lonergan, *Method in Theology*, 58.
43. Lonergan, *Method in Theology*, 58–59.
44. Lonergan, *A Second Collection*, 160. It should come as no surprise that Lonergan adopted Schutz's definition of immediacy and mediation as he referred to "considering any factor, property, aspect to be immediate in one location and mediated in other locations. See *Philosophical and Theological Papers 1958–1964*, 176.

Bernard Lonergan

In "The Mediation of Christ in Prayer," after having laid out several lower kinds of mediation—mechanical, organic, psychic, and logical –, which are not relevant for our present purposes, Lonergan characterizes human growth as a process of self-mediation empowered by existential decisions. "As a community mediates itself by its history, so the individual mediates himself, manifests himself objectively to others and to himself."[45]

In addition to self-mediation, there is *mutual* self-mediation. "Revealing it [one's self-discovery] is an act of confidence, of intimacy, of letting down one's defenses, of entrusting oneself to another. . . . We are open to the influence of others, and others are open to influence from us."[46] So self-mediation can happen "through another," since it is "personal development in relation to another person."[47] However, mutual self-mediation goes further. It amounts to experiences of goodwill and intimacy in which two—or more—individuals influence each other for the better. In other words, persons are assisted by other persons in their respective human development.

In a section of *Method in Theology* titled "Horizons," Lonergan tells us that a horizon comprises people's knowledge and interests. He puts it this way:

> The scope of our knowledge and the range of our interests are bounded. As fields of vision vary with one's standpoint, so too the scope of one's knowledge and the range of one's interests vary with the period in which one lives, one's social background and milieu, one's education and personal development. . . . What lies beyond one's horizon is simply outside one's knowledge and interests: one neither knows nor cares. But what lies within one's horizon is in some measure, great or small, an object of interest and of knowledge.[48]

---

45. Lonergan, *Philosophical and Theological Papers 1958–1964*, 173.
46. Lonergan, *Philosophical and Theological Papers 1958–1964*, 174 and 175.
47. Lonergan, *Philosophical and Theological Papers 1958–1964*, 180.
48. Lonergan, *Method in Theology*, 221–22.

He proceeds to say that "differences in horizon may be complementary, or genetic, or dialectical." For example:

> Workers, foremen, supervisors, technicians, engineers, managers, doctors, lawyers, professors have different interests. They live in a sense in different worlds. Each is quite familiar with his own world. But each also knows about the others, and each recognizes the need for the others.... Such horizons are complementary.[49]

Almost all I have expounded so far has to do with complementary horizons, the meeting of which constitutes the first steps in dialogue. Nevertheless, it is useful to take into consideration the genetic differences in horizon. "They are related as successive stages in some process of development. Each later stage presupposes earlier stages, partly to include them and partly to transform them."[50] Thus someone whose horizon is small may have some difficulty in understanding and even in getting interested in someone else's greater horizon.

What will be ever more demanding is spotting the antithetical differences. "Horizons may be opposed dialectically. What in one is found intelligible in another is unintelligible. What for one is true for another is false. What for one is good for another is evil."[51] And Lonergan is not sanguine about such discrepancies, as he spells out their frequent outcome, "The other's horizon, at least in part, is attributed to wishful thinking, to an acceptance of myth, to ignorance or fallacy, to blindness or illusion, to backwardness or immaturity, to infidelity, to bad will, to a refusal of God's grace."[52]

Notwithstanding such stalemates, Lonergan highlights the great advantage of dialogue: "Encounter . . . is meeting persons, appreciating the values they represent, criticizing their defects, and allowing one's living to be challenged at its very roots by their

---

49. Lonergan, *Method in Theology*, 222.
50. Lonergan, *Method in Theology*, 222.
51. Lonergan, *Method in Theology*, 222.
52. Lonergan, *Method in Theology*, 222.

words and by their deeds."[53] And throughout his works, he insists on the to and fro of question and answer, not only in the sciences and in philosophy, but also in interpersonal encounters.

Comparing Lonergan with Schleiermacher

At this stage it will be beneficial to introduce five comparisons between Schleiermacher and Lonergan, hoping they will be enlightening.

First, we have no evidence of any significant influence by the former on the latter when *Insight* was composed.[54] Nevertheless Lonergan comes very close to Schleiermacher's hermeneutical view as he states that it operates as "a pair of scissors". He explains that "the possibility of any interpretation whatever implies an upper blade of generalities; and the existing techniques of scholars supply a lower blade by which the generalities can be determined with ever greater accuracy."[55] He emphasizes "the significance of the upper blade of method" as follows: "For that upper blade forces out into the open the fact that the proximate sources of meaning lie in the interpreter's own experience, understanding, and judgment."[56]

With the addition of the metaphor of the pair of scissors, this view at least partly amounts to what Schleiermacher characterized as the "universal element" and the "particular element," the first being called "grammatical interpretation" and the second being called "technical" or "psychological interpretation," as we noticed in our preceding chapter. On this point, however, Lonergan's epistemology goes deeper than Schleiermacher's, even though the latter declared that "hermeneutics is a part of the art of thinking."[57]

53. Lonergan, *Method in Theology*, 232.

54. Throughout the 875 pages of *Insight*, there are only a few lines on Schleiermacher, at 701, about a different issue.

55. Lonergan, *Insight*, 600.

56. Lonergan, *Insight*, 603.

57. Schleiermacher, *Hermeneutics*, 97.

Second, another difference between Schleiermacher's and Lonergan's accounts of interpretation is that the former appears somewhat more optimistic concerning particular interpretative instances whereas the latter is more realistic as he draws attention to the difficulty for the interpreters to spot the biases in both themselves and their sources. Schleiermacher nonetheless writes: "The goal of technical interpretation can only be approximated. Despite all our progress we are still far from the goal. . . . Not only do we never understand an individual view (*Anschauung*) exhaustively, but what we do understand is always subject to correction."[58] This continual effort requires that one should be able to find and resolve contradictions, be they dogmatic or historical.[59]

In this respect Lonergan says that "the spontaneous and self-correcting process of learning is a circuit in which insights reveal their shortcomings by putting forth deeds or words or thoughts, and through that revelation prompt the further questions that lead to complementary insights."[60]

Third, Schleiermacher was convinced that text-understanding must build on an earlier step, namely a preliminary knowledge of human beings and a preliminary knowledge of the subject matter. Lonergan's starting point is similar, although it is more resolutely epistemological. Indeed his foundation stems from a self-knowledge that is explicated in an accurate description of the fourfold human intentionality as cross-cultural. This self-knowledge issues forth into a cognitional theory that gives rise to a critical realism and that has a universal validity.

Fourth, both Schleiermacher and Lonergan ascribe a restricted function to logic. The former writes, "For a long time it [general hermeneutics] was treated as an appendix to logic, but since logic is no longer seen as dealing with applied matters, this can no longer be done."[61] The latter writes, "A transition [from

---

58. Schleiermacher, *Hermeneutics*, 149.

59. Schleiermacher, *Hermeneutics*, 88–89.

60. Lonergan, *Insight*, 197.

61. Schleiermacher, *Hermeneutics*, 96; I have rectified the spelling of "logic," which, in English, does not begin with a capital letter, whereas the German

logic] to method, then, does not mean the omission of logical operations, but the explicit additions of other activities such as inquiry, observations, discovery, experimentation, verification."[62] These thinkers acknowledge that logic is indispensable if a thinker wants to spot contradictions and introduce clarifications; however, both also assert that the art of interpretation requires the practice of other, more concrete, operations.

Fifth, Schleiermacher remarked that "the interpreter can put himself 'inside' the author" in order to get to "understanding an author better than he [the author] understands himself."[63] In his Foreword to a book written by David Tracy, Lonergan wrote: "In our many conversations he has let me experience Schleiermacher's paradox, namely, that an intelligent interpreter will know the process of a writer's development better than the writer himself."[64] This experience took place with Tracy, and it appears to have been ideal, so it ought not to be generalized.

Moreover a similar praise for interpreters came from Ricœur, who declared: "To understand an author better than he could understand himself is to display the power of disclosure implied in his discourse beyond the limited horizon of his own existential situation."[65] He also avowed: "My readers have more right than I to interpret [the evolution of my thought], because they have a certain distance from where they can see the entirety of my philosophical work."[66]

Concluding Remarks

In this chapter I have endeavored to exhibit the ways in which Lonergan employed a cognitional theory with its four levels of

---

"Logik" does, as all nouns do.
    62. Lonergan, *Method in Theology*, 345–46.
    63. Schleiermacher, *Hermeneutics*, 64; see 112.
    64. Tracy, *The Achievement of Bernard Lonergan*, xii.
    65. Ricœur, *Interpretation Theory*, 93.
    66. Ricœur," *Between Suspicion and Sympathy*, 671 (reported by Raynova).

intentionality, a sense of historical interpretation, and a dialectic, so as to offer a complex hermeneutical method. Accordingly I presented his epistemology, his functional specialties as constitutive of theological method, his two exposés on interpretation, his dialectic, his conviction that historicity was central in philosophy and in theology, his resulting rejection of extrinsicism, his understanding of interpersonal dialogue as essential for fruitful cooperation in theological work, and finally a comparison between his thought and Schleiermacher's thought on hermeneutics.

6

Paul Ricœur

Paul Ricœur (1913–2005) offers us a wealth of subtle analyses and of successive syntheses. In a previous book, I have presented several of those analyses and syntheses, which it would not be helpful to repeat now.[1] I will focus now on aspects of his thought that are useful for our methodological quest. And since he straddles the fields of phenomenology and hermeneutics, this chapter will start with his phenomenological method and will continue with his expansions, first, from experience to text, and second, from text to action, so that the final primacy of action has become one of the principal themes of my book. Let us note also that none of those expansions amounts to a complete relinquishment of the method that precedes; each development in his thinking subsumes his former position.

The Phenomenological Method

As G. B. Madison rightly said, "in his first major work, *Le Volontaire et L'involontaire* (1950), he sought to expand the phenomenological eidetic method [namely Husserl's method] in such a way

---

1. See Roy, *Revelation in a Pluralistic World*, 145–77.

as to enable it to deal with such noncognitive aspects of human being as volition, emotion, the body, and action."[2] Walter Lowe explained that "*Fallible Man* understands itself as an exercise in 'phenomenology': that is, the work tries simply to *describe* experience, without forcing the description to conform to extraneous suppositions."[3] By "extraneous suppositions," Lowe meant the suppositions of a pre-given philosophy with a prior conception of what human experience must be. In fact, Ricœur always payed sustained attention to the unavoidable presuppositions of any author.

However the significance of truth is not unimportant for Ricœur (who was a committed Protestant throughout his life). He remarked:

> But it has not been possible to limit ourselves to such understanding *of* symbols in symbols. There the question of truth is unceasingly eluded. Although the phenomenologist may give the name of truth to the internal coherence, the systematicity, of the world of symbols, such truth is truth without belief, truth at a distance, reduced, from which one has expelled the question: do *I* believe that? What do *I* make of these symbolic meanings, these hierophanies? That question cannot be raised as long as one remains at the level of comparativism, running from one symbol to another, without oneself being anywhere. That level can only be an intermediate stage, the stage of understanding in extension, panoramic understanding, curious but not concerned. It has been necessary to enter into a passionate, though critical, relation with the truth-value of each symbol.[4]

We must take account of the centrality of symbols in phenomenology. Symbols are figures, often allegorical, such as Satan,

---

2. Hahn, ed., *The Philosophy of Paul Ricœur*, 76. This work should not be confused with *The Philosophy of Paul Ricœur: An Anthology of His Work*, ed. Charles E. Reagan and David Stewart, with same title but a subtitle in the latter.

3. Lowe, Introduction to Ricœur, *Fallible Man*, xix.

4. Ricœur, *The Symbolism of Evil*, 353–54. For discussions of Ricœur's subtle position on truth, see Roy, *Revelation in a Pluralistic World*, 148–49, 155, 162, 166, and 171–74.

Paul Ricœur

Adam, Eve, Abraham, the king, the sorrowful servant, the Son of Man, the second Adam; they are also states, which are not allegorical, such as evil, exile, sin, stain, defilement, guilt, judgment. As types, they all represent something other than themselves, that is, archetypal dispositions, attitudes, deeds, or consequences. Here is Ricœur's definition of the symbol, which he italicized:

> *I define "symbol" as any structure of signification in which a direct, primary, literal meaning designates, in addition, another meaning which is indirect, secondary, and figurative and which can be apprehended only through the first.* This circumscription of expression with a double meaning properly constitutes the hermeneutic field.[5]

Still, another phase follows the reception of symbols, the phase of "reflective philosophy," which amounts to self-knowledge. In that post-symbolic phase, Ricœur acknowledged as valid Descartes' "first truth," namely "I think, therefore I am." Nonetheless he added that it "remains as abstract and empty as it is unassailable. It must be 'mediated' by representations, actions, works, institutions, and monuments which objectify it."[6] However, reflective philosophy ought not to try and translate symbolic expressions into univocal assertions; such a reduction would amount to a loss of semantic wealth.

Religious language is filled with symbols, and symbols are polysemic and therefore complex, since they carry more than one sense. Ricœur defined "multiple meaning" as "a certain meaning effect, according to which one expression, of variable dimensions, while signifying one thing at the same time signifies *another* thing without ceasing to signify the first."[7] Nevertheless, not any meaning is apposite: "But it is the contextual function of discourse to screen, so to speak, the polysemy of our words and to reduce the plurality of possible interpretations, the ambiguity of discourse resulting from the unscreened polysemy. And it is the function of

---

5. Ricœur, *The Conflict of Interpretations*, 12–13.
6. Ricœur, *The Conflict of Interpretations*, 327.
7. Ricœur, *The Conflict of Interpretations*, 63.

dialogue to initiate this screening function of the context."⁸ Consequently, critical though it is, reflective philosophy can show itself to be, in the end, restorative of meaning.

Ricœur stressed the role of three kinds of mediation in interpretation. First, there is the mediation by *signs*, since "it is language that is the primary condition of human experience." Second, there is the mediation by *symbols*, which mediate between the reader and the world. Third, there is the mediation by *texts*, about which we shall say more in our next section.⁹

Right from his tripartite *Philosophie de la volonté*, Ricœur privileged "understanding" (*compréhension*) over "explanation" (*explication*) in his phenomenology; for him, the former belongs in philosophy while the latter belongs in the social sciences (principally psychology and sociology). However, he later became more explicit about a complementarity, namely a "dialectic," as he terms it, between explanation and understanding (*alias* interpretation) even in philosophy.¹⁰ Calling "interpretation" the kind of understanding that hermeneutics applies to texts, he rightly contends that "it seems possible to situate explanation and interpretation along a unique *hermeneutical arc* and to integrate the opposed attitudes of explanation and understanding within an overall conception of reading as the recovery of meaning."¹¹

Ricœur's distinction between explanation (practised by the sciences) and understanding (*alias* interpretation) is enlightening. For him, however, there is a complementarity between these two kinds of thinking. Insofar as philosophy and theology are concerned, it is important not to reduce them to the status of explanation, because we would deprive them of their hermeneutical identity.

Thus phenomenology is richer provided it is construed in terms of hermeneutics, and vice versa, hermeneutics ever remains in need of phenomenology. Ricœur used the comparison of grafting, "Hermeneutics must be grafted onto phenomenology," and

---

8. Ricœur, *Interpretation Theory*, 17.
9. See Ricœur, *From Text to Action*, 16–17.
10. See Ricœur, *From Text to Action*, 125 and 142–43.
11. Ricœur, *From Text to Action*, 121; see 124.

both are transformed in that process.¹² So they are inseparable. On the one hand, talking about "the phenomenological presupposition of hermeneutics," he asserted: "The most fundamental phenomenological presupposition of a philosophy of interpretation [*alias* hermeneutics] is that every question concerning any sort of 'being' [*étant*] is a question about the meaning of that 'being'. . . . *The choice in favor of meaning is thus the most general presupposition of any hermeneutics.*" On the other hand, talking about "the hermeneutical presupposition of phenomenology," he asserted: "By hermeneutical presupposition, I mean essentially the necessity for phenomenology to conceive of its method as an *Auslegung*, an exegesis, an explication, an interpretation."¹³

Ricœur asked, "What prompts 'religious' discourse—as a symbolic mode—toward 'theological clarification'?" His answer is premissed upon the distinction between a first and a second level of discourse. He tells us that it is important to make room for "a second-level reference, which is properly the metaphorical reference."¹⁴ The reference characteristic of the first kind of discourse (ordinary descriptive discourse) does not apply to the second kind of discourse (the genre characteristic of literary creation). Taking seriously the unique nature of the literary work entails adopting a more fundamental mode of reference. Put otherwise, "a new vision of reality springs up, one which is resisted by ordinary vision tied to the ordinary use of words. Then it is the function of poetic language to weaken the first-order reference of ordinary language in order to allow this second-order reference to come forth."¹⁵

The Expansion from Experience to Text

Another important principle of interpretation for Ricœur was *textuality*. Even though existential phenomenology remained the

---

12. Ricœur, *The Conflict of Interpretations*, 17.
13. Ricœur, *The Conflict of Interpretations*, 38 and 43.
14. Ricœur, *The Rule of Metaphor*, 221.
15. Ricœur, "Biblical Hermeneutics," 84.

unsurpassable prerequisite for hermeneutics, the latter was no longer construed as expressing human experience, but rather an attentiveness to texts. As the structure of a text is comprehended, that is, when the internal relations of its synthesis are put together, a text is configured and takes on its meaning.

Ricœur disagreed with "the Romantic tradition [of Schleiermacher and Dilthey] in hermeneutics, which took the dialogical situation as the standard for the hermeneutical operation applied to the text."[16] Whereas Dilthey confused the oral (dialogical) situation with the speaking-hearing situation, Ricœur wanted to show the originality of the latter, which is neither oral nor dialogical.

This explains why Ricœur denied the need to ascertain that which was the intention of a deceased author. In this regard, perhaps a remark by Lonergan could be useful: "Plato and Aquinas and Kant keep on speaking for themselves each in several widely different manners when they are allowed to do so by different interpreters. Nor is this surprising, for they are long dead, and their speaking for themselves is just a metaphor."[17] However, notwithstanding the fact that authors are no longer available to explain orally what they meant, it is not useless to try and inquire into their intention as they composed any particular text, especially when they expressly stated it.

So, what Ricœur proposed was that an author's intention is subordinated to the objective of the text. Thus he said: "By 'autonomy' I understand the independence of the text with respect to the intention of the author, the situation of the work and the original reader." This is a consequence of the fact that "the writing-reading relation is not a particular case of the speaking-hearing relation which we experience in the dialogal situation."[18] As Frederick Lawrence aptly put it, "We experience our world as worded: Our world is always foregrounded for us through interpretations."[19]

---

16. Ricœur, *From Text to Action*, 157.
17. Lonergan, *Insight*, 606.
18. Ricœur, *Hermeneutics and the Human Sciences*, 165.
19. Lawrence, *The Fragility of Consciousness*, 240.

Paul Ricœur

Nonetheless both Schleiermacher and Ricœur asserted that interpreting involves an interaction between something more general and something more particular. Said Ricœur: "The relation of part to whole is ineluctably circular. The presupposition of a certain whole precedes the discernment of a determinate arrangement of parts; and it is by constructing the details that we build up the whole."[20] Moreover meanings must be situated within a whole that includes texts and contexts. Wrote John Thompson:

> The text is a work of discourse, and hence in the first instance a *work*. To say that a text is a work is to say that it is a structured totality which cannot be reduced to the sentences whereof it is composed. Such a totality is produced in accordance with a series of rules which define its literary genre, and which transform discourse into a poem, a novel, a play. At the same time as a work belongs to a genre, so too it has a unique configuration which defines its individual style.[21]

According to his hermeneutical method, Ricœur differentiated two successive steps: "I used the term 'configuration' to refer to the internal organization of the type of discourse being examined—in that case, narrative—and I called 'refiguration' the effect of discovery and transformation this discourse brings about in the hearer or reader through the process of receiving the text."[22]

The Expansion from Text to Action

Another important principle of interpretation is the *action* that brings back any reading to reality. In his 1995 "Intellectual Autobiography," Ricœur explained:

> In two different ways, the movement from the text to action was produced by the theory of the text itself: either

---

20. Ricœur, *Hermeneutics and the Human Sciences*, 175.

21. Editor's introduction, in Ricœur, *Hermeneutics and the Human Sciences*, 13.

22. Ricœur, *The Whole and Divided Self*, 204.

> the intersubjective relation inherent in the discourse reorients the analysis toward the practical world of the reader which the text redescribes or refigures, or the referential relation, no less essential to the full exercise of discourse, makes us attentive once more to the primacy of acting and suffering being included within that of the being-to-be-said in relation to being.[23]

The proposed, projected world is not a fact, but rather a possible world, a world to be. What is at stake here for interpretation? Ricœur thus elaborated: "The question of language is thus no longer simply a milieu in which a discourse on action can be articulated; it is a mode of being, a pole of existence as fundamental as action itself."[24]

> What is to be interpreted in a text is a proposed world, a world that I might inhabit and wherein I might project my ownmost possibilities. This is what I call the world of the text, the world probably belonging to this unique text.... Fiction and poetry intend being, but not through the modality of givenness, but rather through the modality of possibility.[25]

Similar assertions can be found in the Conclusions of *Time and Narrative*:

> Reading becomes a provocation to be and to act differently. However this impetus is transformed into action only through a decision whereby a person says: Here I stand!... Narrativity is not denuded of every normative, evaluative, or prescriptive dimension.... Still it belongs to the reader, now an agent, an initiator of action, to choose among the multiple proposals of ethical justice brought forth by reading. It is at this point that the notion of narrative identity encounters its limit and has to

---

23. Ricœur, *The Philosophy of Paul Ricœur*, 38.

24. Ricœur, Foreword to Don Ihde, *Hermeneutic Phenomenology*, xiv.

25. Ricœur, *Figuring the Sacred*, 43. As the subtitle (*Religion, Narrative, and Imagination*) indicates, imagination (in its usual broad sense) is central in this delineation of "a proposed world"; see Ricœur, *From Text to Action*, 168–87.

link up with the nonnarrative components in the formation of an acting subject.[26]

As a result, the meanings of actions are never fixed:

> Like a text, human action is an open work, the meaning of which is "in suspense." It is because it "opens up" new references and receives fresh relevance from them, that human deeds are also waiting for fresh interpretations that decide their meaning. All significant events and deeds are, in this way, opened to this kind of practical interpretation through present *praxis*.[27]

Ricœur's final enterprise focused on action, namely on a pragmatics. In addition to semantics, which deciphers the literal meaning of words, pragmatics attends to the broader meaning perceived by the speaker and the listener, who both pay attention to the mode, the place, and the time of utterances so as to create meaning.

Always keeping in mind his fascination for language, Ricœur nevertheless repeatedly nuanced it by stating that "discourse is an action" and "human action is a speaking action."[28] Furthermore it is still within the context of narratives that, towards the end of his long career, he developed an ethics: "By placing narrative theory at the crossroads of the theory of action and moral theory, we have made narration serve as a natural transition between description and prescription."[29]

Ricœur's pronounced accent on the evolving senses of texts by no means entailed a negligence of reality, and especially of humanness; he is keen to equally underscore "the 'redescription' of human reality."[30] Surely, "to interpret is to explicate the kind of being-in-the-world displayed *before* the text. What is then submitted to interpretation is the *pro-position* of a world in which I could dwell, a world created by the projection of my own utmost

26. Ricœur, *Time and Narrative*, vol. 3, 249.
27. Ricœur, *From Text to Action*, 155.
28. Ricœur, *Figuring the Sacred*, 305.
29. Ricœur, *Oneself as Another*, 170.
30. Ricœur, "Biblical Hermeneutics," 33; he borrowed the term "re-description" from Mary Hesse (see 85).

possibilities."³¹ We belong in a world, but not according to all our desires. He added:

> This implies that the reader does not submit the meaning of the text to his own finite capacity of understanding, but that he lets himself be exposed to the text, in order to receive from it a *Self*. By *Self* I mean a non-egoistic, non-narcissistic, non-imperialistic mode of subjectivity, which responds and corresponds to the power of a work to display a *world*.³²

As a result "the intentionality of the work as a whole" has as "its intention to represent human actions as higher than they are in reality."³³

Such a project does not come about in a facile way. One has to face up to conflicting interpretations and, to do so, one has to practise a distanciation. Thus Ricœur emphasized the indispensable role of distanciation with regard to initial interpretations; distanciation "is linked to any objective and objectifying study of a text." And yet this concept is accompanied by a "counterpart, namely "the concept of appropriation."

> Appropriation is the concept which is suitable for the actualisation of meaning as addressed to someone. It takes the place of the answer in the dialogical situation, in the same way that 'revelation' or 'disclosure' takes the place of ostensive reference in the dialogical situation. The interpretation is complete when the reading releases something like an event, an event of discourse, an event in the present time.³⁴

Further on in the same article, Ricœur had these words of caution:

---

31. Ricœur, "Philosophical Hermeneutics and Theological Hermeneutics," 25.
32. Ricœur, "Philosophical Hermeneutics and Theological Hermeneutics," 30.
33. Ricœur, *Hermeneutics and the Human Sciences*, 180.
34. Ricœur, *Hermeneutics and the Human Sciences*, 185.

Paul Ricœur

"Relinquishment is a fundamental moment of appropriation and distinguishes it from any form of 'taking possession.' Appropriation is also and primarily a 'letting-go.' Reading is an appropriation-divestiture." He added, "Only the interpretation which satisfies the injunction of the text which follows the 'arrow' of meaning and endeavors to 'think in accordance with' it, engenders a new *self*-understanding."[35]

Consequently a definite suspicion is in order in the hermeneutical attitude towards the self. Suspicion is triggered by "the recognition of an *external* adversary, whom one does not attempt to retrieve and baptize by force, and also become the instrument of an *internal* critique, which appropriately belongs to the labour of distantiation [sic] which all self-understanding before the text requires." Therefore "a 'hermeneutics of suspicion' is an integral part of all appropriation of meaning. And with it follows the 'deconstruction' of prejudgments which impede our letting the world of the text be."[36]

The hermeneutics of suspicion is followed by the hermeneutics of recovery (*alias* recollection or restoration). One justifiably passes from "the first faith of the simple soul" to a "second faith" or "postcritical faith" which "seeks, through interpretation, a second naiveté," namely a "recovery," a "recollection," or a "restoration of meaning" in their response to the great religious texts.[37] Great texts contain a potential for reexamination of one's life, reorientation, and personal conversion. Nevertheless such an interpretative venture is more promising when it is done in community, according to tradition, and with discernment, given the presence of conflicting views.[38] This interpersonal requirement of the intellectual life—and of life tout court—is conspicuous in his Gifford Lectures.[39]

35. Ricœur, *Hermeneutics and the Human Sciences*, 191 and 192–93.
36. Ricœur, *From Text to Action*, 32.
37. Ricœur, *Freud and Philosophy*, 28.
38. Ricœur, "Discussion d'ensemble," 228.
39. His first ten Gifford Lectures were published as *Oneself as Another*, whose reference I gave in an earlier footnote; his eleventh lecture appeared in *The Whole and Divided Self*, 201–20; and his twelfth lecture appeared in *Figuring the Sacred*, 262–75.

Concluding Remarks

Ricœur observed, "Hermeneutics is the theory of the *operations* of understanding in their relation to the interpretation of texts."[40] After Schleiermacher and Lonergan, he felicitously spoke of "operations" as he characterized hermeneutics' procedures. It was thanks to a continuing succession of different intellectual activities, ever prompted by novel questions, that he offered to numerous people such rich philosophical views.

I hope that this chapter has substantiated the claim that I am making now, that Ricœur was one of the leading, if not the leading, hermeneut of the twentieth century, as Augustine was the greatest hermeneut of Antiquity.[41]

---

40. Ricœur, *From Text to Action: Essays in Hermeneutics, II*, 53; italics added.

41. In *Augustin dans la pensée de Paul Ricœur*, Isabelle Bochet specified Augustine's influence, which Ricœur had received from his great predecessor. I am indebted to my friend James Pambrun for having me find this book.

8

Yves Congar and Claude Geffré

This last chapter will complete our book with two other hermeneutical contributions, one by Yves Congar and the other by Claude Geffré. The former passed away in 1995 and the latter in 2017. Both were French Dominicans and both acknowledged their gratitude to Thomas Aquinas's way of thinking, which I presented in chapter 4.

Yves Congar, Historian and Thinker

Yves Congar surely is a model for apprentices in theology.[1] Two authors of a book on him noticed his flexibility over the years:

> A fascinating aspect of this great theological figure [was] his capacity to evolve serenely and to publicly acknowledge that evolution by correcting some of his anterior positions, in the manner of St. Augustine's famous *retractationes* or auto-criticisms.... No Copernican revolution, certainly, in his theological thought, but an evolution that was progressive and permanent, intelligent, courageous

---

1. For a survey of Congar's theological concerns and achievements, see Le Guillou, "Yves Congar."

and loyal, implying a constant spiritual contact with his times, his Church and the other Churches.[2]

Our two authors mentioned a host of factors that facilitated Congar's evolution and brought about a broadening of his viewpoint: attentiveness to reality (*le réel*) of the Church and of the world, to history and life, return to the historical sources, the practice of ecumenism.[3]

In the course of the Second Vatican Council, during which he played a very important role, Congar made a successful defence of the historical method, with which he had become acquainted thanks to Marie-Dominique Chenu, his teacher in France.[4] He noted that in the late-nineteenth and early-twentieth centuries, the scholastic manuals used in the Catholic Church were ruled by a sort of static logic that prevented the understanding of the Christian realities.[5]

Moreover the authors of those manuals seemed to be unaware of what the Second Vatican Council taught about the hierarchy of truths.[6] Congar spoke of a "hierarchy of truths" (*hiérarchie des vérités*), with, as a synonym, "arranging of truths" (*échellonnement des vérités*). He also wrote: "If there exists a hierarchy among truths, it is first of all in the realities. Certainly, it is only there because the Uncreated Spirit of God ("Veritas Prima") has conceived realities to be in such a way. The hierarchy of truths is implanted in the realities by divine knowledge."[7]

Additionally it is worth taking account of Congar's distinction between Tradition (singular and with a capital T) and traditions

---

2. Famerée and Routhier, *Yves Congar*, 8. Apart from Congar's and Geffré's texts that have been published in English, the translations are mine.

3. Famerée and Routhier, *Yves Congar*, 176–77.

4. At the house of studies of the French Dominicans, called "Le Saulchoir," Chenu considerably influenced Congar, his pupil, regarding the notion of historicity, See Roy, "The Significance of Human Historicity for Marie-Dominique Chenu and Bernard Lonergan," forthcoming in The Lonergan Review.

5. See Congar, *A History of Theology*, chaps. 4–6.

6. See "Decree on Ecumenism" (*Unitatis Redintegratio*), §11.

7. See Congar, "The Hierarchy of Truths," 126–33.

(plural and with a small t).[8] On that distinction, I commented in an earlier book: "Usually, a theologian operates within one tradition; sometimes, however, great minds manage to reconcile varied intellectual traditions without confusion, for example Aquinas, who admirably synthesized Neoplatonism and Aristotelianism while managing to circumvent eclecticism." I added, "Recognizing this distinction between Tradition and traditions may exercise a liberating effect by making sure a particular tradition is not a dead letter, but a healthy interpretation that is alive, namely friendly to future articulations."[9]

However we must acknowledge that it is not easy to identify or redefine the Tradition amidst the numerous traditions; we need a flexible and concerted endeavor on the part of several scholars who are listening to many voices such as those of catechists, poets, artists, musicians, and ordinary people.

Congar actualized a kind of dynamic historical thinking. As early as 1967, that is, two years after the Second Vatican Council, he praised the then current renewal of theology that consisted in "the awareness that theologians acquired, not only of the real state of the world from the point of view of faith, but of their role towards this situation."[10] He went on by mentioning (1) the phenomenological method and the philosophy of existence, which emphasized the difference between the human person and the world of things; (2) an intersubjective or interpersonal ontology; and (3) the historicity of the human condition.[11]

For instance both in the first edition and in the second, revised, edition of *Vraie et fausse réforme dans l'Église* (1950 and 1968), he deplored the fact that "Catholic theology has devoted little study to the life of the Church. . . . In general, Catholic theology has given little consideration to Christian realities as experienced

---

8. See Congar, *Tradition and Tradition*. The issue of Tradition/tradition has been discussed in terms of content/context by Guarino, *Foundations of Systematic Theology*, 145–53 and 188–94.

9. Roy, *Revelation in a Pluralistic World*, 212.

10. Congar, *Situation et tâches présentes de la théologie*, 16–17.

11. Congar, *Situation et tâches présentes de la théologie*, 17–18.

by religious subjects." (By "subjects" he meant "persons.") He mentioned as exceptions "Möhler and Newman, two great minds who were precisely the ones to introduce into theology a consideration both of the religious subject and of historical development." So he argued in favor of "a theology of the *life* of the Church, that is, of the Church insofar as it is also made up of human beings."[12] Elsewhere he explained human subjects' historicity in these simple words: "Humankind makes itself, the world makes itself every day. Throughout advances and regressions, successes and failures, the detours and zigzags of a polyvalent history, a world seeks itself and gives birth to itself, a humanity forms itself."[13]

He also gave this insistent advice:

> Instead of starting only from what is given in Revelation and Tradition, as classical theology [after the Council of Trent] has generally done, we must start from facts and questions received from the world and from history. This is much less comfortable. We cannot be content any more to repeat what is old by starting from the ideas or problems of the thirteenth or sixteenth centuries. We must start from the problems, if not the ideas, of today and take them as a new 'given.' The unchanging 'given' of the Gospel must then shed its light on the new given without the support of the elaborations achieved in the past and possessed in the calm of an assured tradition.[14]

Congar declared, in an interview:

> Having too many certainties may stop questions from emerging before they are even formulated whereas to live the questions is a source of fruitfulness. . . . I reproach myself sometimes for not sufficiently living the questions, for cutting them off too quickly with answers. Under these conditions, they might only be the answers to the questions

---

12. Congar, *True and False Reform in the Church*, 9, 10, and 11. I have slightly modified the translation.

13. Congar, *À mes frères*, 79. By "frères" he meant all Christians, namely, in today's parlance, his brothers and sisters.

14. "Situation et tâches présentes de la théologie," 9,), 2; I made one modification in the translation.

of the day before yesterday, or yesterday, but maybe not answers to the questions of today or tomorrow.[15]

Underlying these accents is the presence of the human subject as a writer, a speaker, a reader, a listener, or as a person we have known directly or indirectly. Brother Émile, of Taizé, the author of a study on Congar's thought, wrote: "His [Congar's] conception of Tradition made much room for human experience, for the singularity of every experience, and therefore it is welcoming toward a contemporary disposition and longing. For Congar, the subject is a constitutive principle of truth."[16]

Congar himself remarked:

> It is not enough to say that there is a living subject; it must be added that this subject lives *in history* and that historicity is one of its inherent features, without, however, implying that its truth is relative or that it is nothing more than the successive and changing thought of men.[17]

Brother Émile rightly insisted on the centrality of the Holy Spirit in Congar's life and work: "To this sense of dialogue, to this capacity to live the questions without rushing to answer them, and to this openness to what is new and unknown, we should add Congar's ever-growing attention to the person and the role of the Holy Spirit in the Church." Brother Émile mentioned Congar's three-part volume on the Holy Spirit, his last major book.[18] And he commented:

> His achievements cannot be explained solely by his outstanding intellect. His deep spiritual life—a true life in the Spirit—and his attention to the person and to the role of the Holy Spirit in the life of the Church were determining factors. Until the end of his life Congar remained a man of prayer. His theological œuvre is that of an apostle.[19]

15. *Jean Puyo interroge le Père Congar*, 238–39.
16. Brother Émile, *Faithful to the Future*, 37.
17. Congar, *The Meaning of Tradition*, 114.
18. See Congar, *I Believe in the Holy Spirit*.
19. Brother Émile, *Faithful to the Future*, 30–31.

Methodologies in Systematic Theology

I have quoted Brother Émile because I am hoping that my readers would clearly resonate with the utmost importance of relying on the Holy Spirit for all of us who wish to implement a multidimensional method in theology. Therefore, in order to identify, on a topic of faith, the Tradition amidst various traditions, we need the Holy Spirit's prayed-for assistance, solid historical information, paying serious attention to our contemporaries' questions and convictions, and sound intellectual judgment. I think that Congar possessed and employed those four resources.

Talking about a rosy view of evangelization, which conceals the obstacles met in dialogue, he expressed this warning:

> Prejudices are more difficult to extirpate than that, and they *also* exist in those who carry the Gospel, who had to or ought to carry it. Things do not happen as in a fairy tale. The Church lives historically, she experiences a real history. She experiences true emerging dramas, as all dramas, opposition from free wills, resistance of the flesh to the spirit, limitations, lack of knowledge and at times human stupidity.[20]

We need to pay attention to a problematic issue that Congar raised a couple of years after the end of Vatican II. Having mentioned the variety of theological systems, for instance about the differences between Aquinas's and Bonaventure's kinds of thought, Congar, in an Addendum to one of his books, expressed doubts concerning Maritain's opinion that Thomism could integrate elements of twentieth-century philosophies. He said, "The optimistic idea of a complementarity that would allow a superior synthesis is applicable only to pieces, not to the totality in which an intuition systematically expressed itself." He immediately added that "the non-synthetizable" does not mean "the contradictory," and he cited, as evidence, his experience with his Orthodox friends.[21]

In the rest of his Addendum, Congar voiced three conditions for a productive theological work. First, patience within an unconditional love and patience for truth, along with an absolute trust

---

20. Congar, *Cette Église que j'aime*, 93.
21. Congar, *Situation et tâches présentes de la théologie*, 82.

in it; second, a reciprocal openness that excludes no research, that knows and is interested in other scholars' research, with mutual cooperation and critique, in a spirit of welcoming and hospitality; and third, honoring the primacy of the realities of the faith over the representations, conceptualization, expressions and systematizations into which we can try to translate and construct those realities.[22] Although Bernard Lonergan did not often quoted Congar, he would agree with these three conditions, while he would insist on developing a more critical methodology—something we are going to find in Geffré.

Claude Geffré, Expert in Theological Hermeneutics

Whereas Congar expressed mostly *psychological* conditions for fruitful research, Geffré tackled mostly *intellectual* conditions, although the former was aware of the intellectual conditions while the latter was aware of the psychological conditions. I am speaking of "intellectual conditions" as being not merely theoretical, but as including also existential factors. Thus Geffré's hermeneutical search was always a real personal quest for God.[23]

Moreover, without explicitly referring to Congar, Geffré concurred with the latter on the necessity for theologians to foster a theology of the life of the Church, as we noted above. In an early work he wrote, "As an actualization of the Word of God, theology is faithful to its task only if the life of the Church in a specific situation constitutes for it a privileged locus of the Christians' praxis."[24] Needless to say, according to both Congar and Geffré this process of actualization must be continual and endless, so as to fulfill its role in the Church.

---

22. Congar, *Situation et tâches présentes de la théologie*, 82–83.
23. See Geffré, *Un espace pour Dieu* and *Profession Théologien*.
24. Geffré, *A New Age in Theology*.

Methodologies in Systematic Theology

Interestingly Congar held Geffré's oeuvre as being "d'un très beau metal," that is, "of the highest quality."[25] Nevertheless Geffré went farther than Congar in his reflections on hermeneutics. This was in part due to his sustained attention to Ricœur's works, mostly to the latter's insistence, which we noted in our chapter on Ricœur *the philosopher*, on beginning the interpretative work with classical texts.[26] For Geffré *the theologian*, it meant beginning the interpretative work with Holy Scripture and continuing with the gathering of subsequent texts included in a very broad hermeneutical field that embraces numerous traditions, ancient and novel, emanating from both Christians and non-Christians.

Moreover he pointed out that *within* the New Testament there is a distance between the events that are reported about the pre-Easter Jesus and the interpretation conferred upon them by his disciples' post-Easter faith. Consequently, over two millennia interpreters have had the delicate task of re-interpreting for their time what had already been an interpretation, namely the New Testament itself. So in addition to the *within*, the successive followers of Jesus, Christ and Lord, have engaged into a *without*, for they have had to take into consideration two hermeneutical tensions, one within the revelatory text itself, and one that had to quickly happen later in the process of adapting—while not reducing—the Good News to various cultures.[27]

So, for Geffré there must be a mutual influence between the signs of the times (= human experience) and the voices of the Bible and the Christian traditions (= revelation). He thus rectified Paul Tillich's method of correlation, which presented human experience as raising questions, and revelation as providing the answers. In sound practice, then, the very framing of the questions is modified by revelation, and the interpretation of the answers is

---

25. Congar, in the Avant-Propos of *Interpréter*, 9. One day, showing me his copy of Geffré's *Un nouvel âge de la théologie*, Lonergan told me he thought that it was a very good book.

26. Allusion to Ricœur are numerous in Geffré's post-1980 writings.

27. See Geffré, "L'herméneutique chrétienne," in *L'état des religions dans le monde*, 451.

modified by human experience.²⁸ Hence we have here a reciprocal and critical correlation. Therefore, warns Geffré, we must avoid a lopsidedness either in a reading of Scripture that makes little of human experience and, as a result, is theologically self-sufficient, or in granting to human experience a prevalence over Scripture.²⁹

Geffré praised the Second Vatican Council's mention of the "signs of the times" and Chenu's elaboration of those signs. Chenu had given, as instances, "the decolonization, the unification of the world, the plurality of civilizations, the evolution of the ways of working, and the access of the popular masses to a political consciousness."³⁰ Geffré's list, which he termed "states of consciousness," is similar; it includes: "a sense of conscience's autonomy, the aspiration to happiness, the person's dignity and the worth of human life, the democratic conception of life in society, the right to religious freedom, and the acceptance of pluralism."³¹ Later he added "a new attentiveness to the values of sexuality," "the place of women in society" and "the possibility not only to fight against the evil that is illness, but to try and find the means of a greater wellbeing."³² Elsewhere he mentioned other important signs of the times as "the encounter between the religions"³³ and "the fundamental equality among human beings."³⁴

Of course neither Chenu nor Geffré meant to be exhaustive in their lists. However, whereas the former was immoderately optimistic in the contents of his list, the latter was more restrained, as he showed a greater awareness of the twentieth-century horrors,

---

28. See Geffré, "La théologie au sortir de la modernité," 290–91. This point was very well made by Richard's chapter, "La théologie comme herméneutique chez Claude Geffré et Paul Tillich." For information on the same point, see Pambrun, "Hermeneutical Theology and Narrative," 289 with its long footnote 61, 297–98, and 301.

29. Geffré, "Révélation et expérience historique des hommes," 10.

30. *Jacques Duquesne interroge le Père Chenu*, 71. Chenu provided a similar list at 126.

31. Geffré, "Révélation et expérience historique des hommes," 13.

32. Geffré, *Profession Théologien*, 194.

33. Geffré, *De Babel à Pentecôte*, 15–25.

34. Geffré, *Le christianisme comme religion de l'Évangile*, 55.

Methodologies in Systematic Theology

such as the catastrophic wars and the Jewish genocide. He declared: "Taking the risk of interpreting Christianity means reinterpreting again and again the good news of salvation in the light of this counter-experience of the great and world-wide suffering of contemporary mankind. I am saying this here to forestall a cricicism that my approach is hypercritically intellectual."[35] Much later, he asserted, "Human history, particularly in the twentieth century, is, above all, the history of the disfiguring of man."[36]

According to Geffré's practice, there must be a critical reading of several kinds of documents: biblical pronouncements concerning the faith experience (in the First and in the New Testament), authoritative renderings of various Christian and non-Christian religious traditions (among which Geffré had chosen Islam), and the multifarious construals by theologians of the equally multifarious instances of contemporary experience.

Geffré also sided with a good number of thinkers who rightly considered the inclusion of practical reflections in the mission of theology or of philosophy of religion and of politics. Gadamer called this task "application"; Ricœur said, according to Geffré's paraphrasing, that "the world of the text, indeed, induces the subject into actualizing its most proper possibilities in order to transform the world"; Jean Ladrière promoted a "coadaptation between an interpretative system and a system of action."[37] What these three philosophers enunciated was taken up by Geffré, who wrote:

> If we are willing to define theology as hermeneutics, we must see that it is indissociable from an unceasing dialectic between theory and practice. It does not rest content with proposing a new interpretation of Christianity. It takes seriously the concrete [human] subjects of history and normally leads to a "doing," to a certain

---

35. Geffré, *The Risk of Interpretation*, 7.

36. Geffré, *Le christianisme comme religion de l'Évangile*, 154.

37. Geffré, "L'entrée de l'herméneutique en théologie," 262; it was a lecture he had given at the one-hundred anniversary of the Institut catholique de Paris. See his whole article, 245–71, from which I drew several considerations for this section on Geffré.

transformation of the social practice of human beings in the expectation of the coming Kingdom.[38]

Felicitously Geffré balanced this practical function of texts with their poetical, celebratory, and meditative character. He stated that we need this resource so as to counter the "growing domination of the technical-economic powers that invade all the spheres of our social, cultural, and medias-run life."[39] Nonetheless one can wonder why, with his strong emphasis on texts, he omits the importance of *oral* dialogue in mutual quests for meaning and truth. Doesn't even the sound of someone's voice evidence something significant?

To conclude this section: As he was praising the "incarnation of the Word of God in human words . . . in the reality of the mind," Geffré declared:

> Faith never eliminates the regime of the mind, since it can only be *understood* according to that regime. This quasi-axiom has been for me the guide of my theological life. This amounted to try and live faith in a regime that was the one of modernity, and at the same time to re-translate the Christian message so that it would be received.[40]

To conform to that "regime of the mind," one must cultivate "a new self-understanding."[41] It is therefore important not to try and make sense of biblical wisdom without also engaging into philosophical self-knowledge—a point that both Lonergan and Ricœur stress, as we noted in our preceding chapters. Nonetheless, thanks to the Bible and the fundamental Christian experience, the great font of certainty is the First Truth that Aquinas highlights as central to faith. In an interview, Geffré confided:

> I learned from Thomas Aquinas that theologal faith owns the homage of its obedience only to the very authority of

---

38. Geffré, "La théologie au sortir de la modernité," 201; see his whole article, 189–209.
39. Geffré, "L'entrée de l'herméneutique en théologie," 271.
40. Geffré, *Profession Théologien*, 73.
41. Geffré, *Croire et interpréter*, 35.

God as *First Truth*. This was the secret of my interior liberty when I did not always see the link between certain truths taught by the Magisterium of the Church and the truths that belong to Revelation proper.[42]

Actually Geffré acknowledged that serious and dedicated theological involvement entailed facing the danger of making mistakes; I would add, not in Christian faith itself, but in any construal of Christian faith. He avowed: "The word 'risk' is ambivalent. In speaking of the risk of interpretation, the reader should not forget that I am also speaking of the risk of distortion and error. In the case of Christianity, there is an even greater risk—that of faith itself."[43]

This risk is inevitably concomitant with creativity, namely with "the risk of a creative interpretation of the Christian message." He explained:

> The misuse of the word 'creative' can hide our powerlessness to explore the riches of the past. But when I speak of creative interpretation, I am not thinking of the misuse of an interpretation claiming to come from nothing. I am thinking more of a resumption without repetition of the Christian message, which is only faithful to itself insofar as it produces new historical figures in the form of writings or original practices.[44]

Concluding Remarks

Both Congar's and Geffré's accented the great importance of historicity, which they inherited from Chenu. Nevertheless, notwithstanding Congar's general appreciation for Geffré, mentioned at the beginning of my section on the latter, it must be acknowledged

---

42. Geffré, *Le christianisme comme religion de l'Évangile*, 295. Aquinas asserts this point at the very beginning of his treatise on faith, in the *Summa Theologiae*, that is, at II–II, q. 1, a. 1; see Roy, *The Three Dynamisms of Faith*, 75–83.

43. Geffré, *The Risk of Interpretation*, 1.

44. Geffré, *The Risk of Interpretation*, 3.

that the former, being involved, from 1965 until 1995, in major historical researches and in multiple interventions about the relevance of Vatican II, did not significantly engage into explicating the issues raised by modern hermeneutics—issues that commenced to be addressed in Catholic *theology*—of course not altogether in Catholic *circles*—approximately around 1980.

Geffré was the main exponent of those issues and he recognized his passion for contemporary philosophy, especially hermeneutics, and for Martin Heidegger's philosophy. To the question put by an interviewer, "had it been proposed that you engaged into philosophy," he confessed: "Intellectually so, probably. I enjoy philosophy, and I acknowledge that the practice of philosophy is a practice more free than the one exercised by theology, especially when one has to teach that which one must write."[45] By contrast, Congar confessed, "I am no philosopher. I lack that capacity for philosophic reflection which enables the possessor to deepen concepts and to systematize thoughts."[46]

While, to my knowledge, Congar did not discuss epistemology and metaphysics, Geffré expressly rejected metaphysics. He explained his stand as follows:

> Understood as hermeneutics, theology takes account of the rupture with metaphysical thought as the thought of representation, but it does not give up the ontological scope of the theological enunciations. . . . We do not dispense with ontology. . . . Rather we seek to take seriously the ontology of language in the line of the second Heidegger and the second Ricœur.[47]

Unfortunately Geffré did not distinguish between Aquinas's metaphysics and modern-scholastic metaphysics, thus following Heidegger's attack on any metaphysics, beginning with Plato's

---

45. Geffré, *Profession Théologien*, 66; on his interest in Heidegger's philosophy, see 68.

46. Congar, "Reflections on being a Theologian," 409.

47. Geffré, *Croire et interpréter*, 18. A long treatment of metaphysics can be found in his *A New Age in Theology* (1972 in the French edition), especially in chapter 3, and it recurred often in his teaching and publications.

metaphysics.[48] We have here a contrast between Geffré and Lonergan, who, in his book *Insight*, justified the existence of Aquinas's metaphysics and made it understandable by connecting it to intellectual self-knowledge.[49] That is to say, without dismissing metaphysics, Lonergan resituated it within the scope of what he baptized "cognitional theory." So he wrote:

> The basic terms and relations of systematic theology will be not metaphysical, as in medieval theology, but psychological. . . . General basic terms name conscious and intentional operations. General basic relations name elements in the dynamic structure linking operations and generating states. Special basic terms name God's gift of his love and Christian witness. Derived terms and relations name the objects known in operations and correlative to states. The point to making metaphysical terms and relations not basic but derived is that a critical metaphysics results.[50]

Nevertheless since Congar and Geffré learned much from Thomas Aquinas, obviously there is a certain Thomist continuity between the two of them, although there is a *dis*continuity with the *modern* scholasticism that I portrayed in chapter 1.

---

48. Regarding Heidegger on this point, see Roy, *God: Polarities in Language*, forthcoming, section titled "Heidegger's Rejection of Metaphysics." Geffré had in mind metaphysics as "representation" (the very word he used); however the medievalist Édouard-Henri Wéber told me one day that the primacy of the representation can be traced back to Henry of Ghent, followed by Duns Scotus and the whole crowed of modern scholastics. For more on this view, which Lonergan called "conceptualism," see Roy, "Bernard Lonergan's Construal of Aquinas's Epistemology."

49. See Lonergan, *Insight*, 343–617.

50. Lonergan, *Method in Theology*, 317. Perhaps Geffré would have been sympathetic to this notion of a *critical* metaphysics, but to my knowledge he *never* quoted Lonergan.

Conclusion

Genuine Christians have always been eager to seek an understanding of their faith, be it rudimentary or sophisticated: *fides quaerens intellectum*, as St. Anselm put it. In line with today's approach to this enterprise, we could say that the desire to understand better what we believe leads to inculturation, namely to expressing the Good News in the categories found in several cultures.

Notwithstanding this goal, which is common to all Christian theologians, their overal kinds of thinking have varied a great deal. So let me differentiate them into three basic styles: (1) mainly symbolic and about one aspect of Christianity; (2) holistic and covering a few aspects of Christianity; and (3) mainly conceptual with a rational control of meaning. The first genre consists of symbolic presentations accompanied by a minimum of conceptual explanations; the second genre consists of general visions of what Christianity is and of how it can be correctly interpreted; the third genre amounts to systematic understandings of what Christianity is.

Here are instances of each genre: (1) The apostolic Fathers (end of first century and the first half of the second century; (2) Irenaeus of Lyon (end of the second century), Basil of Caesarea and Gregory of Nyssa (fourth century), Karl Barth, Hans Urs von Balthasar, Yves Congar, Paul Ricœur and Claude Geffré (twentieth century); and (3) Gregory of Nazianzen (fourth century), Augustine of Hippo (beginning of the fifth century), Maximos the Confessor (seventh century), John of Damascus (early eighth century), Thomas Aquinas (thirteenth century), Schleiermacher (first half of the nineteenth century), Karl Rahner and Bernard Lonergan (twentieth century).

We have also noted several modern authors' nuanced assessment of historicity, which fashions an enormous variety of cultures. This sense of history allows scholars to appreciate both the particular and the permanent in religious studies that convey meanings. Moreover, as we saw in the present book, a person's sense of history includes the endeavor to make a difference in history itself. If we think again about the authors whose thought we have examined, all of them were convinced of the duty to influence human history, some of them implicitly (Augustine, Albert, Thomas, Schleiermacher, Congar), others explicitly (Ricœur, Lonergan, Geffré).

The arduous task of interpretation cannot be an individualistic one. It ever demands an interaction with other people, who express their views orally or in writings.[1] Whatever their methodologies are, they have been and are fashioned in dialogue. Hence the saying, "no one is an island." The constant challenge thus consists in correctly interpreting others, either in person or through their texts. It requires the reading, not of very few theologians, but of a good number of them with a great variety of thinking style.[2]

Furthermore all the authors on whom I wrote a chapter were intensely concerned with the mentalities, namely the *Zeitgeist* of their time. For Augustine, the problem was a wrong understanding of love in the heresies of the Pelagians, the Donatists, and the pagan thinkers who opined that the Christians were guilty for the fall of the Roman Empire; for Aquinas, the principal representative of a serious intellectual challenge to the Christian faith was Aristotle; for Schleiermacher, those he wanted to attract to Christianity were "the cultured despisers" of religion; for Lonergan, the readers he

1. Please allow me to refer again to my piece titled "Principles of Fruitful Interreligious Dialogue."

2. While Lonergan detailed the practice of dialogue (see the section titled "Interpersonal Dialogue" in chapter 6 of the present book), Congar and Geffré said only a few words about their agreement with this requirement. I had the personal experience of listening to, and of being listened to, by each of them.

Conclusion

targeted were those who ignored Catholic philosophy; for Ricœur, the adversaries were the French structuralists; for Congar, the partners in dialogue were the Protestants and the Orthodox; for Geffré, the principal error he countered was the structuralists (and indirectly the Neo-Thomists) who had banished both historicity and hermeneutics from philosophy and theology. Needless to say, all of those thinkers were keenly interested in numerous sources of learning, even the sources coming from their opponents—a clear sign of their openness of mind and of their boldness.

I would end this book by giving this advice: "For fresh and novel insights on many issues, read Augustine, the great insightful; and for detailed evaluations of, frequently, the same issues, read Aquinas, the great synthesizer." And to pursue this contrast a bit further, I would say: "For an insistence on 'either/or,' read Augustine; and for an insistence on 'both/and,' read Aquinas. The former lived in a time where it was necessary to complete the sorting-out of Christian doctrines because several of them had remained somewhat unclear; the latter lived in a time where it was necessary to interlink the doctrines systematically, for the sake of a vaster understanding of them, especially in connection with secular reason.

There is no serious theology without puzzlement and hard thinking; all other elaborations of doctrines are stale and fruitless. The pitfall, for believers, is to merely *repeat* the final synthesis of an Aquinas or of some other dogmatic thinker, sometimes while moving around or modifying its pieces. By contrast, the right way of theologizing is to retrace the steps of an Augustine, an Aquinas or someone else, to personally and freshly re-appropriate the dynamic flow of inquiry, to relive the paradoxes and tensions that must precede any resolution.[3]

---

3. This is what I tried to do, in discussion with stimulating thinkers, in my forthcoming book *God: Polarities in Language*, chap. 1, titled "Divine Attributes in Tension."

Bibliography

Aristotle. *Nicomachean Ethics*. Translated by Terence Irwin. Indianapolis, IN: Hackett, 1999.
Augustine. "The Advantage of Believing" (*De utilitate credendi*), in *On Christian Belief*. Translated by Ray Kearney. Hyde Park, NY: New City Press, 2005.
———. *Against the Academics*, Translated by John J. O'Meara. New York: Newman Press, 1951.
———. *The Confessions*. Translated by Maria Boulding. Hyde Park, NY: New City Press, 2nd ed., 2012.
———. *The First Catechetical Instruction* (*De Catechizandis Rudibus*). Translated by Joseph P. Christopher. New York: Newman Press, 1946.
———. *The Greatness of the Soul* (*De quantitate animae*). Translated by Joseph M. Colleran. New York: Newman Press, 1964.
———. *Homilies on the Gospel of John*. Translated by Edmund Hill. Hyde Park, NY: New City Press, 2020.
———. *Responses to Miscellaneous Questions*. Translated by Boniface Ramsey. Hyde Park, NY: New City, 2008.
———. *Sermons III/3 (51–94) on the New Testament*. Translated by Edmund Hill. Brooklyn, NY: New City Press, 1990.
———. *Sermons III/6 (184–229A) on the Liturgical Seasons*. Translated by Edmund Hill. New Rochelle, NY: New City Press, 1993.
———. *Sermons III/10 (341–400) on Various Subjects*. Translated by Edmund Hill. Hyde Park, NY: New City Press, 1995.
———. *Teaching Christianity* (*De Doctrina Christiana*). Translated by Edmund Hill. Hyde Park, NY: New City, 1996.
———. *The Trinity* (*De Trinitate*). Translated by Edmund Hill. Brooklyn, NY: New City Press, 1991.
Bevans, Stephen B. *Models of Contextual Theology*. Maryknoll, NY: Orbis, 2002.
Blondel, Maurice. *Action (1893): Essay on a Critique of Life and a Science of Practice*. Translated by Oliva Blanchette. Notre Dame, IN: University of Notre Dame Press, 1984.
Bochet, Isabelle. *Augustin dans la pensée de Paul Ricœur*. Paris: Facultés Jésuites, 2004.

Bibliography

———. "*Le firmament de l'Écriture*": *L'herméneutique augustinienne*. Paris: Institut d'études augustiniennes, 2004.

Boff, Clodovis. *Theology and Praxis: Epistemological Foundations*. Translated by Robert R. Barr. New York: Orbis Books, 1987.

Braaten, Carl E. "The Heritage of Dogmatics," in volume 1 of *Christian Dogmatics*. Edited by Carl E. Braaten and Robert W. Jenson. Philadelphia: Fortress Press, 1984.

Brother Émile, of Taizé, ed. *Faithful to the Future: Listening to Yves Congar*. London: Bloomsbury, 2013.

Calvin, John. *Institutes of the Christian Religion*. Translated by Henry Beveridge. Grand Rapids, MI: Eerdmans, 1989.

Congar, Yves. *À mes frères*. Paris: Cerf, 1968.

———. *Cette Église que j'aime*. Paris: Cerf, 1968.

———. "The Hierarchy of Truths," in *Diversity and Communion*. New London, CT: Twenty-Third Publications, 1985.

———. *A History of Theology*. Translated by Hunter Guthrie. Garden City, NY: Doubleday, 1968.

———. *I Believe in the Holy Spirit*. Translated by David Smith. New York: Herder and Herder, 1997.

———. *The Meaning of Tradition*. Translated by A. N. Woodrow. San Francisco: Ignatius Press, 2004.

———. *Situation et tâches présentes de la théologie*. Paris: Cerf, 1967.

———. *Tradition and Traditions: An Historical and a Theological Essay*. Translated by Michael Naseby and Thomas Rainborough. New York: Macmillan, 1966.

———. *True and False Reform in the Church*. Translated by Paul Philibert. Collegeville, MN: Liturgical Press, 2011.

De Chardin, Teilhard. *The Phenomenon of Man*. Translated by Bernard Wall. New York: Harper & Row, 1965.

Dunn, James D. G. *A New Perspective on Jesus*. London: SPCK, 2005.

Duquesne, Jacques. *Jacques Duquesne interroge le Père Chenu: "Un théologien en liberté"*. Paris: Centurion, 1975.

Frei, Hans W. *Types of Christian Theology*. Edited by George Hunsinger and William C. Placher. New Haven, CT: Yale University Press, 1992.

Gadamer, Hans-Georg. *Truth and Method*, 2nd English ed., revised by Joel Weinsheimer and Donald G. Marshall. New York: Crossroad, 1991.

———. *"Who Am I and Who Are You?" and other essays*. Translated by and Edited by Richard Heinemann and Bruce Krajewski. Albany, NY: SUNY Press, 1997.

Geffré, *De Babel à Pentecôte: Essais de théologie interreligieuse*. Paris: Cerf, 2006.

———. *Le christianisme comme religion de l'Évangile*. Paris: Cerf, 2012.

———. *Croire et interpréter: Le tournant herméneutique de la théologie*. Paris: Cerf, 2001.

———. "L'entrée de l'herméneutique en théologie," dans *Les cent ans de la faculté de théologie*. Edited by Joseph Doré. Paris: Beauchesne, 1992.

Bibliography

———. *Un espace pour Dieu*. Paris: Cerf, new rev. ed., 1996.

———. "L'herméneutique chrétienne," in *L'état des religions dans le monde*, Edited by Michel Clévenot. Paris: Cerf, 1987.

———. *A New Age in Theology*. Translated by Robert Schillemn and others. New York: Paulist Press, 1974.

———. *Profession Théologien: Quelle pensée chrétienne pour le XXIe siècle?* Paris: Albin Michel, 1999.

———. "Révélation et expérience historique des hommes." *Laval Théologique et Philosophique* 46 (1990): 3–16.

———. *The Risk of Interpretation: On Being Faithful to the Christian Tradition in a Non-Christian Age*. Translated by David Smith. New York: Paulist Press, 1986.

———. "La théologie au sortir de la modernité," in *Christianisme et modernité*, Edited by Roland Ducret and others. Paris: Cerf, 1990), 290–91.

Giambrone, Anthony. *A Quest for the Historical Christ: Scientia Christi and the Modern Study of Jesus*. Washington, DC: Catholic University of America Press, 2022.

Griffiths, Paul. "The Limits of Narrative Theology," in *Faith and Narrative*. Edited by Keith E. Yandel Oxford: Oxford University Press, 2001), 217–36.

Grondin, Jean. *Introduction to Philosophical Hermeneutics*. Translated by Joel Weinsheimer. New Haven, CT: Yale University Press, 1994.

Guarino, Thomas G. *Foundations of Systematic Theology*. New York: T&T Clark, 2005.

Gutiérrez, Gustavo. *A Theology of Liberation: History, Politics, and Salvation*. Translated by Sister Caridad Inda and John Eagleson. Maryknoll, NY: Orbis Books, rev. ed., 1988.

Heide, Gale. *Timeless Truth in the Hands of History: A Short History of System in Theology*. Cambridge, UK: James Clark, 2012.

Henn, William. "Hierarchy of Truths," in *The New Dictionary of Theology*, Edited by Joseph A. Komonchak, Mary Collins and Dermot A. Lane. Wilmington, DE: Glazier, 1987), 464–66.

Irenaeus, *Adversus Haereses*, in vol. 1 of *The Ante-Nicene Fathers*. Grand Rapids, MI: Eerdmans, 1977.

Kant, Immanuel. *Grounding for the Metaphysics of Morals*. Translated by James W. Ellington. Indianapolis, IN: Hackett, 1993.

Lawrence, Frederick G. *The Fragility of Consciousness: Faith, Reason, and the Human Good*. Edited by Randall S. Rosenberg and Kevin M. Vander Schel. Toronto: University of Toronto Press, 2017.

Le Guillou, M.-J. "Yves Congar," in *Bilan de la théologie au XXe siècle*. Edited by R. Vander Gucht and H. Vorgrimler. Tournai: Casterman, 1971), vol. II, 791–895.

Lonergan, Bernard. "Beyond Extrinsicism and Immanentism," in *Early Works on Theological Method 1*, CWBL, vol. 22. Edited by Robert M. Doran and John D. Dadosky. Toronto: University of Toronto Press, 2010.

Bibliography

———. *Insight: A Study of Human Understanding*. Collected Works of Bernard Lonergan (henceforth CWBL), vol. 3. Edited by Frederick E. Crowe and Robert M. Doran. Toronto: University of Toronto Press, 1992.

———. *Method in Theology*. CWBL, vol. 14. Edited by Robert M. Doran and John D. Dadosky. Toronto: University of Toronto Press, 2017.

———. "The Method of Theology Spring 1963," in *Early Works on Theological Method 3*, CWBL, vol. 24. Translated by Michael G. Shields and edited by Robert M. Doran and H. Daniel Monsour, Toronto: University of Toronto Press, 2013.

———. *A Second Collection*. CWBL, vol. 13. Edited by Robert M. Doran and John D. Dadosky. Toronto: University of Toronto Press, 2016.

———. *Philosophical and Theological Papers 1958–1964*, CWBL, vol. 6. Edited by Robert C. Croken, Frederick E. Crowe, and Robert M. Doran, Toronto: University of Toronto Press, 1996.

———. *A Third Collection*, CWBL, vol. 16. Edited by Robert M. Doran and John D. Dadosky. Toronto: University of Toronto Press, 2017.

G. B. Madison, "Ricœur and the Hermeneutics of the Subject," in *The Philosophy of Paul Ricœur*. Edited by Lewis Edwin Hahn. Chicago: Open Court, 1995.

Manning, Patrick R. *Converting the Imagination: Teaching to Recover Jesus' Vision for Fullness of Life*. Eugene, OR: Pickwick, 2020.

Marcel, Gabriel. *Homo Viator: Introduction to a Metaphysic of Hope*. Translated by Emma Craufurd. London: Victor Gollancz, 1951.

———. *The Mystery of Being*, vol. 2, *Faith and Reality*. Chicago: Regnery, 1960.

Maréchal, Joseph. *A Maréchal Reader*. Translated by Joseph Donceel. New York: Herder, 1970.

———. *Le point de départ de la métaphysique*. Paris: Desclée de Brouwer: L'édition universelle, 2nd ed., 1937.

Henri-Irénée Marrou. *Saint Augustin et la fin de la culture antique*. Paris: De Boccard, 4th ed., 1958.

McEvenue, Sean E., and Ben F. Meyer, eds. *Lonergan's Hermeneutics: Its Development and Application*. Washington, DC: Catholic University of America Press, 1989.

Meier, John P. *A Marginal Jew: Rethinking the Historical Jesus*. New York: Doubleday, vol. 1, 1991.

Meyer, Ben F. *The Aims of Jesus*. London: SCM Press, 1979; reprint at Eugene, OR: Wipf and Stock, 2002.

———. *Critical Realism and the New Testament*. Allison Park, PA: Pickwick, 1989.

———*Reality and Illusion in New Testament Scholarship: A Primer in Critical Realist Hermeneutics*. Collegeville, MN: Liturgical Press, 1994.

Neuner, J., and J. Dupuis, eds. *The Christian Faith in the Doctrinal Documents of the Catholic Church* .New York: Alba House, rev. ed., 1982.

Newman, John Henry. *An Essay in Aid of a Grammar of Assent*. Edited by I. T. Ker. Oxford: Clarendon Press, 1985.

Bibliography

———. *An Essay on the Development of Christian Doctrine*. Edited by Mary Katherine Tillman. Notre Dame, IN: University of Notre Dame Press, 1989.

Niebuhr, H. Richard. *Christ and Culture*. New York: Harper & Row, 1951.

Oakes, Edward T. "Apologetics and the Pathos of Narrative Theology." *The Journal of Religion* 72 (1992), 37–58.

Pambrun, James R. "Hermeneutical Theology and Narrative." *Theoforum* 32 (2001): 273–301.

Puyo, Jean. *Jean Puyo interroge le Père Congar: Une vie pour la vérité*. Paris: Centurion, 1975.

Rahner, Karl. *Foundations of Christian Faith: An Introduction to the Idea of Christianity*. Translated by William V. Dych. New York: Crossroad, 1984.

Raynova, Yvanka B. "All that Gives us to Think: Conversations with Paul Ricœur," in *Between Suspicion and Sympathy: Paul Ricœur's Unstable Equilibrium*. Toronto: Hermeneutic Press, 2003.

Richard, Jean. "La théologie comme herméneutique chez Claude Geffré et Paul Tillich," in *Interpréter: Hommage amical à Claude Geffré*. Edited by Jean-Pierre Jossua and Nicolas-Jean Sed. Paris: Cerf, 1992, 69–101.

Ricœur, Paul. "Biblical Hermeneutics," *Semeia* 4 (1975): 84.

———. *The Conflict of Interpretations: Essays in Hermeneutics*. Edited by Don Ihde. Evanston, IL: Northwestern University Press, 1974.

———. "Discussion d'ensemble," in Ricœur and others. *La Révélation* Bruxelles: Facultés universitaires Saint-Louis, 1977, 15–54.

———. *Fallible Man*. Translated by Charles A. Kelbley, New York: Fordham University Press, rev. trans., 1986.

———. *Figuring the Sacred: Religion, Narrative, and Imagination*, Translated by David Pellauer and edited by Mark I. Wallace. Minneapolis: Fortress Press, 1995.

———. Foreword to Don Ihde, *Hermeneutic Phenomenology: The Philosophy of Paul Ricœur*. Evanston, IL: Northwestern University Press, 1971.

———. *Hermeneutics and the Human Sciences*. Translated by John B. Thompson. Cambridge, UK: Cambridge University Press, 1981.

———. "Intellectual Autobiography," in *The Philosophy of Paul Ricœur*. Edited by Lewis Edwin Hahn. Chicago: Open Court, 1995.

———. *Interpretation Theory: Discourse and the Surplus of Meaning*. Forth Worth: Texas Christian University Press, 1976.

———. *Oneself as Another*. Translated by Kathleen Blamey. Chicago: University of Chicago Press, 1992.

———. "Philosophical Hermeneutics and Theological Hermeneutics." *Studies in Religion/Sciences Religieuses* 5 (1975): 14–33.

———. *The Rule of Metaphor: Multi-disciplinary Studies of the Creation of Meaning in Language*. Translated by Robert Czerny with Kathleen McLaughlin and John Costello. Toronto: University of Toronto Press, 1977.

Bibliography

———. "The Self in the Mirror of the Scriptures." Translated by David Pellauer, in *The Whole and Divided Self*. Edited by David E. Aune and John McCarthy New York: Crossroad, 1997.

———. *The Symbolism of Evil*. Translated by Emerson Buchanan (Boston: Beacon Press, 1969.

———. *From Text to Action: Essays in Hermeneutics, II*. Translated by Kathleen Blamey and John B. Thompson. Evanston, IL: Northwestern University Press, 1991.

———. *Time and Narrative*. Translated by Kathleen McLaughlin and David Pellauer. Chicago: University of Chicago Press, 3 vols., 1984–1985.

———. *The Voluntary and the Involuntary*. Translated by Erazim V. Kohák Evanston, IL: Northwestern University Press, 1966.

Roy, Louis. "Bernard Lonergan's Construal of Aquinas's Epistemology." *Method: Journal of Lonergan Studies*, New Series 8 (2017): 17–31.

———. *Engaging the Thought of Bernard Lonergan*. Montreal: McGill-Queen's University Press, 2016.

———. *The Feeling of Transcendence, an Experience of God?* Translated by Pierre LaViolette and Anne Louise Mahoney. Eugene, OR: Wipf and Stock, 2021.

———. *God: Polarities in Language*. Forthcoming.

———. *Meaning in People's Lives and in Human History*. Forthcoming.

———. "Medieval Latin Scholasticism: Some Comparative Features," in *Scholasticism: Cross-Cultural and Comparative Perspectives*. Edited by José Ignacio Cabezón. Albany, NY: SUNY Press, 1998.

———. *Mystical Consciousness: Western Perspectives and Dialogue with Japanese Thinkers*. Albany, NY: SUNY Press, 2003.

———. "Principles of Fruitful Interreligious Dialogue: A Few Suggestions." *Studies in Interreligious Dialogue* 29 (2019): 159–83.

———. *Revelation in a Pluralistic World*. Oxford: Oxford University Press, 2022.

———. "Schleiermacher's Epistemology," *Method: Journal of Lonergan Studies* 16 (1998): 25–46.

———. "Scholasticism," in *Christianity: A Complete Guide*. Edited by John Bowden. London: Continuum, 2005), 1085–88.

———. "The Significance of Human Historicity for Marie-Dominique Chenu and Bernard Lonergan." Forthcoming.

———. *The Three Dynamisms of Faith: Searching for Meaning, Fulfillment and Truth*. Washington, DC: Catholic University of America Press, 2017.

———. "Thomas Aquinas since Vatican II." *The Lonergan Review* 10 (2019): 109–15.

———. *Transcendent Experiences: Phenomenology and Critique*. Toronto: University of Toronto Press, 2001.

———. "The Viability of the Category of Religious Experience in Bernard Lonergan's Theology." *Method: Journal of Lonergan Studies*, New Series 6 (2015): 99–117.

Bibliography

Schleiermacher, Friedrich D. E. *Brief Outline of Theology as a Field of Study: Translation of the 1811 and 1830 Editions.* Translated by Terrence N. Tice Lewiston, NY: Edwin Mellen Press, 1990.
———. *The Christian Faith.* Edited by H. R. Mackintosh and J. S. Stewart Edinburgh: T&T Clark, 1986.
———. *Hermeneutics and Criticism and Other Writings.* Translated by Andrew Bowie. Cambridge, UK: Cambridge University Press, 1998.
———. *Hermeneutics: The Handwritten Manuscripts.* Translated by James Duke and Jack Forstman. Atlanta, GA: Scholars Press, 1977, reprint 1986.
Taylor, Charles. *Philosophical Papers,* vol. 2: *Philosophy and the Human Sciences.* Cambridge, UK: Cambridge University Press, 1985.
Teevan, Donna. *Lonergan, Hermeneutics, & Theological Method.* Milwaukee: Marquette University Press, 2005.
Thomas Aquinas. *Commentary on Aristotle's Nicomachean Ethics.* Translated by C. I. Litzinger. Notre Dame, IN: Dumb Ox, 1993.
———. *Scriptum super Libros Sententiarum.* Edited by Pierre Mandonnet. Paris: Lethielleux, 1929–1948.
———. *Summa contra Gentiles.* Translated by Vernon J. Bourke. Notre Dame, IN: University of Notre Dame Press, 1975.
———. *Summa Theologiae.* Translated by Fathers of the English Dominican Province. 3rd ed., 22 vols. Vol. 1. London: Burns, Oates and Washbourne, 1916.
Tracy, David. *The Achievement of Bernard Lonergan.* New York: Herder and Herder, 1970.
Troeltsch, Ernst. *The Social Teaching of the Christian Churches.* Translated by Olive Wyon. Louisville, KY: Westminster/John Knox Press, 1992.
Wilkins, Jeremy. *Before Truth: Lonergan, Aquinas, and the Problem of Wisdom.* Washington, DC: Catholic University of America Press, 2018.

www.ingramcontent.com/pod-product-compliance
Lightning Source LLC
Chambersburg PA
CBHW050834160426
43192CB00010B/2019